what **not** to wear on a horse

what not to wear on a horse

Ginny Oakley and Stephanie Soskin

KENILWORTH PRESS

4

First published in 2005 by
Kenilworth Press Ltd
Addington
Buckingham MK18 2JR

© Ginny Oakley and Stephanie Soskin 2005

British Library Cataloguing in Publication Data
A catalogue record for this book is available from the British Library

ISBN 1-872119-94-8

Design by Paul Saunders
Layout by Kenilworth Press
Printed in Malta on behalf of Compass Press

contents

acknowledgements

Ginny and Steph would like to thank their families and friends, the willing and not-so-willing models, and loyal clients who waited patiently for lessons and missed appointments during the writing of this book. It is worth mentioning our lack of computer skills, so special thanks must go to Adrian (always on the end of the phone to talk us through a computer experience) and Simon and James who aided in setting up computers and saving our work. We have always been afraid of a mouse and still are! Also thanks to Sir Richard Daddy Bayliss for correcting so many literary mistakes.

Our thanks go to all our non-professional models, including Doris the dummy, who did such a great job – David, Paul, Karl, Adrian, Michele, Denise, Helen, Nicky, Yvonne, Hannah (the designer underwear provider), Annabel, Suzanne, Suzie and her children Hermione and Ellamanda, also our model and hairdresser Estelle.

A big thank you to Whittlebury Golf and Country Club where most of the photographs were taken and who looked after us so well.

To Townfield Saddlers who provided many of the clothes used.

Thanks to John Minoprio, the photographer, and Sim who guided us through the pictorial ordeal.

To Kenilworth Press for believing in the idea and gently pushing us to keep to a very tight schedule.

Our special thanks (and a big pat) to the most patient of models, Annie and Coco, our horses, who waited all day to be stars; and to their wonderful grooms Louise and Julie.

introduction

Several books have been written on the subject of correct dress for riders. Mostly they offer guidance on outfits for specific disciplines (showing, hunting, dressage, etc.), but they don't explain **how** to wear the clothing, nor how to choose what's right for **you**, nor, most importantly, advise on what **not** to wear.

To be told that you should wear a tweed jacket for a certain class is all well and good, but what about the cut, colour and fit? Today, there is more choice than ever before: fabrics are superior, different styles abound and colours are plentiful. This is where the problem lies: there is now much more chance to get it wrong – and many riders do!

Designers and manufacturers in the equestrian clothing market are able to cater for all sizes and body shapes. Whether you have a figure of a catwalk model (we hate you) or a page-three girl, or are rounded or vertically challenged, the correct choice of clothes and colour can make all the difference, and you really can look like the 'mutt's nuts'!

We want to spare you the agonies of choosing unsuitable apparel and the embarrassment of being a 'nearly-but-not-quite'. Take it from us – we've been there and done it. Our basic education, like so many, started in the hunting field – and there can be no better place to learn about dress discipline and standards.

Couple this with our ability to move with the times, our show ring experience and our knowledge of the fashion world and saddlery trade, and we believe this puts us in a very good position to pass on sartorial advice.

Prevention is better than cure. We will guide you on how to develop the required image before you buy, thus avoiding expensive mistakes.

Gentlemen, you are not forgotten. Without a doubt, some men look drop-dead gorgeous in their riding kit; and some men, well ... but we are here to help. Yes, like the fairer sex, you come in all sizes, but fear not, the shorter, well-rounded man need not look like Mr Pickwick, and the thinner, leggier version not like Mr Bean! Nureyev breeches need not reveal all, unless you particularly want them to. Read on and take heart.

We have to acknowledge that riding and being around horses is quite a risky business in more ways than one. While we recommend and advise on what to wear, it must be noted that safety standards are constantly being improved and it is up to you to keep up to date so that your welfare is protected.

Horse societies regularly update their health and safety regulations with good cause. Therefore, please make sure that you are correct and abide by the rules of the various disciplines.

You may be interested to learn that a lot of the clothes seen in this book were the models' own or were begged and borrowed. The newer clothes were lent to us by a well-known equestrian supplier.

What body shape are you?

The human body comes in many different shapes and sizes. Most of us would probably like to be a different shape, and certainly as we age and various parts go south, our bodies change but possibly not as we wish. Flat-chested ladies want bigger boobs, the larger ones want a reduction, and men want bigger balls and a six-pack.

Everybody fits into a different body-shape category. There are tall, thin people; tall, fat people; short, fat people; and short, thin people. Then there are pear-shaped, hour-glass, rectangular, and inverted triangle figures. There are people who are big breasted, small breasted, high waisted and low waisted; and there are those with heavy thighs and thick calves.

Only when we truly recognise our own body shape (perhaps with a little help from a friend whom we can rely on to be completely honest, and the use of a very large mirror or two) can we try to dress it accordingly. In fact, very few horse people have ever looked at themselves dressed to ride in a full-length mirror, front and back – so let battle commence!

People who ride regularly tend to be quite athletic. Their back and shoulders tend to be broader than average, the biceps well developed, while the waist, hips and thighs may be small. (Contrary to popular belief, ladies who ride don't always have bigger bums and thighs. These areas do, in fact, get toned up.) Riding clothes have to allow for this, but to get a perfect fit for your riding jacket you may have to undertake some clever nipping and tucking of the clothing, not the body, to produce the desired and attractive effect.

Legs that work hard will be firm and muscular, but not every rider has a perfect pair of pins and a tight bum. No amount of exercise will change your basic leg shape or give you legs up to your armpits, but the correct cut in breeches and boots and the right length of jacket can create a very favourable illusion.

Although riding clothes can be all-revealing, believe us, there are ways to disguise problem areas and enhance your body shape. As a result you can feel less self-conscious about your figure and how you look. We know we can help you make the difference.

one | *hair, make-up and jewellery*

Correct hair and make-up is a must for the lady rider, and in this chapter we will look at ways of avoiding bad hair days, and applying the right sort of finishing touches to equip you with that elegant, effortless look we all strive for.

Hair

There is no doubt that good turn-out needs time, patience and, above all, practice to get it right on the day. Unless you are a wiz at doing fancy hairstyles with any type of hair, we can assure you that making the perfect-sized bun is an art. A bun is not always necessary, unless in side-saddle classes where it is a must, but it does smarten long hair and gives a much neater appearance than a baggy hairnet.

No matter what you are doing; everyone will look at your face, so if the top part of you is a mess, the picture will never be right. Hair and make-up need addressing – but hair in particular, in all riding disciplines, very often leaves a lot to be desired.

For the gentleman rider there are fewer options. To be neat you do have to have shorter hair, although there is nothing wrong with the cut being modern. Added highlights

● nearly but not quite – hairnet is too long, and obvious mistake with ribbons

● bad hair day   ● trying   ● hallelujah!

● modern man with modern hairstyle still looking neat and tidy

can enhance style and colour for both men and women but the horse world is not yet used to seeing crazy colours like red or blue!

The hairstyle you have chosen in everyday life is going to affect how you wear your hair under a hat. If you want to make a bun, you need to be able to fashion your hair into a doughnut size 'ball' that rests just above the nape of your neck and sits on the hair at the back of your head. The ease of this operation will depend a lot on the length and texture of your hair. Hair can be worn over or behind the ears but there must be no wisps peeping out.

Short hair can easily be made to look long with the use of a false bun. These can be made up by your hairdresser or bought from retailers. A similar match in colour is very important. Thin hairnets over your own hair will aid in attaching and holding the false bun in place. Hairpins and Kirby grips are essential, as is a ton of hairspray.

If a bun is not for you, find ways of securing

long or bushy hair before you even start to cram it into a hairnet. Really long hair looks super when put into a long plait and then wound around into a bun shape at the nape of the neck.

Remember that if wearing a safety hat any hairstyle must accommodate the three-point straps.

Scrunchies are good to put over a hairnet to secure medium-length hair in a ponytail. Short hair need only have a hairnet, but do make sure that your hairnet is not bigger than your head and your hair! If using a heavy net, make a knot in it at the front to tighten it. This will ensure that you will lose the extra net that you don't need and it will pull the hair up tighter to the bottom of the hat and create a much neater appearance.

● very neat and tidy hairnet and scrunchie

Children can get away with bunches and long plaits or free ponytails in the show ring. The addition of bows and ribbons is fine as long as their colour matches the outfit and browband, but some parents seem to overdo this and the eye is totally drawn to the hair and not the pony! This loose mass of hair is not looked upon kindly in the dressage arena, and is no longer allowed on the jumping circuit for safety reasons. Lady riders in the

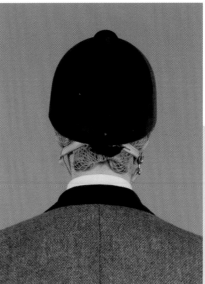

● untidy and common, then correctly shown with shortened hairnet

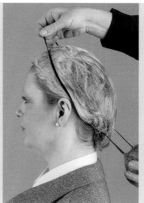

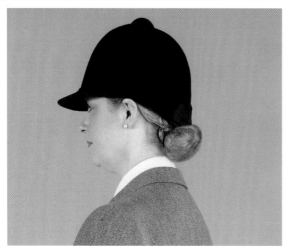

● short hair made long – not a very good match of bun but a stunning end result. this picture also shows good make-up and pearl earrings for daytime wear

USA appear to lose their hair under their hats. This very stylish method is possible as their bespoke hats are measured to accommodate this.

We personally feel that lightweight hairnets look far better than heavy ones, and, if one is not enough, wear two over each other. This will still look far better than one heavy, baggy net. Very short hair may gain little from a hairnet, but do address the hair around your face when under a hat. Hair tucked behind the ears may not stay there without help. Hair spray or wax will aid control immensely.

> ***top tip*** If using a false bun, attach a piece of fine elastic to the bun and wear it around your head under your hat. This is a superb way of making sure you don't leave parts of your attire in the ring after the gallop. Use pins to secure the bun firmly to your own hair – after all, you don't want your bun to move onto the side of your neck so you appear to have the largest, hairiest mole in the world! You need to be thinking about where you are going, not where your hair is going.

Having a bad hair day is simply not an option for the correctly turned out rider.

Mid-length hair can be treated in two ways. Some prefer to pin and tuck it up under the hat and then add a false bun. If there is not enough hair to make a big enough bun, a bun ring can be used.

● many hands make light work – but we promise you can do this on your own!

top tip   Clean, well-conditioned silky hair looks lovely but is terrible for the bun-maker and the hairstylist. If possible, do not wash your hair the day before a show, but if you have to, skip the conditioner.

top tip   If you have wispy hair at the base of the neck, use some hair wax to get it under control. This is far easier and less messy to use than gel.

top tip   The worst thing about wearing a riding hat is what it does to your hair. All riders are only too aware of getting off the horse and walking around the showground with 'hat hair'. Unless you own a really deluxe lorry with jacuzzi and shower, it is rarely an option to wash and blow-dry your hair. A baseball cap or similar is a good option to hide an unkempt barnet. However, there is a way of doing a quick make-over on your hair after riding. If you have a fringe or shorter layers at the crown and these have taken on a life of their own, dampen by hand or, better still, use a water sprayer to lightly wet the offending area. Rub gently with a towel and then keep brushing until some normality is restored. This method has saved both of us many a time from a never-ending bad hair day caused by a hat. Gentleman can also employ this tip .

● do not use this as a reliable form of contraception!

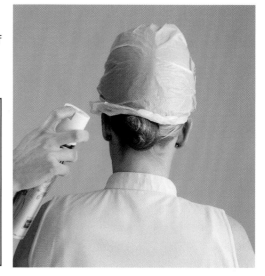

top tip   If you need to add a final touch of hairspray while you are wearing your hat, to avoid wrecking the velvet either pop a plastic bag over your hat or hold a piece of paper over the hat near to where you are spraying. Be very careful not to smother yourself with the plastic bag!

This resembles a spongy doughnut with a hole in the middle through which you put your hair and pin around. Unsurprisingly this takes much practice, but when done well, looks fantastic.

Long hair can be made into a bun with the aid of bun nets, pins and a prayer! Again this needs practice, as there are different methods of making a bun. Security of the hair is essential so always put it into a ponytail first.

Make-up

Very few of us can get away without some help from the make-up department. Certainly, some thoughtfully applied colour can really help your overall appearance.

Too much make-up during the day can lead to a painted-doll look; equally so, an unmade-up face can look pale and stark. If your game is side-saddle riding, remember that without make-up your features may disappear totally under your veil.

If you are about to enter the ring and have turned a whiter shade of pale, a little blusher will take away that startled rabbit look. At the very least, some tinted moisturiser, which is as easy to apply as face cream, and some Vaseline on your lips are better than nothing. (Make sure you keep your Vaseline separate from the pot you use on the horse's nose and bum!)

Concealer is a great ally for getting rid of those bags and dark shadows under your eyes, caused by getting up at the crack of sparrow. Do, if possible, put your foundation and mascara on before you leave the house so as not to frighten other road users. This is one thing you can get done early, before going to work or a show.

It is well documented that women who are dressed well and made up well have greater confidence in themselves. This really does apply to the show ring, and if you would rather blend in with the scenery, then maybe this is not the sport for you. However, there is no reason for the lady show jumper, dressage or event rider not to look her best when competing. Today's make-up is quick and easy to apply, so lack of time is not really an excuse.

 top tip Avoid shiny faces on hot days by using powder. Loose powder is the most effective but too problematic to use around blue and black jackets.

● acceptable daytime make-up for the younger rider

Don't just put on the same colour eye shadow and lipstick that you wear every day – think about your outfit. For example, light blue eye shadow with a green keeper's tweed jacket just does not go. Your lipstick shouldn't clash with your ensemble either – a lady in orange lipstick, wearing a red tie and sitting on a chestnut horse is not exactly pleasing on the eye. You need to think carefully about the colours you want to use and how they will go together.

Most horsey girls are well known for having the worst kept nails, but there really isn't any excuse for this. They polish their horse's feet and spend a small fortune on shoeing, but won't fork out for emery boards. We both manage to have nice nails, even

top tip   Check out the colour of your lipstick against that of your jacket, shirt and tie. Always use a lipstick that you have worn before and that you know does not bleed.

top tip   Riding can be hot work, rain or shine. Always go for powder shadows and waterproof mascara. You will be grateful for run-proof mascara when having an emotional moment because you have won or lost.

top tip   After applying foundation use a wet wipe around and under your jaw line and neck to avoid creepage onto your collar or silk stock.

top tip   For day-time classes, avoid the painted doll or panda look. Very dark or bright lipstick is not a good choice. For evening classes under lights you will, however, need more make-up, as bright, artificial lights will pale any complexion.

top tip   The side-saddle rider will always need that bit extra so she does not become a faceless rider under her veil. Be cautious about using very sticky glossy lipsticks as they tend to have a better affair with your veil than with your lips.

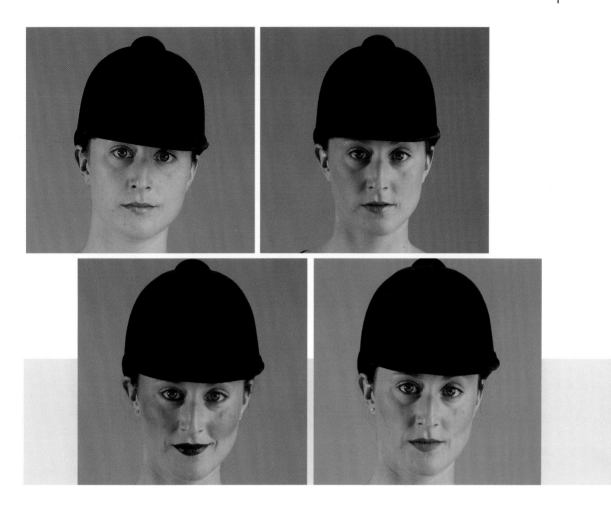

though mucking out is a regular chore and we are not rubber glove ladies! It takes very little time with quick-dry varnishes to add a bit of colour and keep dirt from being seen – very practical! A layer of varnish also protects the nails when doing endless mane and tail washing. A full nail make-over is only necessary once or twice a week, and a touch-up with another coat makes do in between. Chipped nail varnish looks hideous: be prepared – always take nail varnish remover pads or spare polish to touch up or eradicate problems. If polish is not for you, at least try to keep the nails clean and don't bite them!

False nails have made an enormous comeback, even in the horse world, with the introduction of gel and acrylic. Needless to say, both of us have tried these, but with dire consequences. They

● clockwise from top left: naked, day, evening and lap dancer!

do look fantastic and there are riders who are great fans of them. The fact that they can leave your hand while your own nails are still attached to them (ouch!) means we cannot recommend them.

 top tip If you suffer from greasy skin or tend to get very hot, resulting in a shiny face, take a tip from the professional actors of the world. Baby powder brushed on lightly over naked or foundation-covered skin is a great solution to this problem. We do recommend a little blusher afterwards, but the stage professionals find that this really does keep everything in place.

top tip Do not forget to use sun cream for both yourself and your horse – sunburnt, pink noses are not pleasant on man nor beast.

top tip All the make-up advice applies equally to men, but please keep the lipstick to a neutral shade!

Jewellery

For safety reasons we all know that riders should not wear jewellery of any kind. Realistically, this is not the case, and riders, both male and female, are regularly seen wearing the odd bit of 'bling'. Small stud earrings are an attractive choice for the female rider wearing either a strapless riding cap or topper. Rules on this seem to be changing daily, so if you are not sure, take them out. Anything larger looks ghastly, and the fashion of wearing ten earrings in one ear should be saved for nights in the pub. The same can be said for men and earrings, although we see a single earring rather too often nowadays. Hoops or anything dangling look perfectly awful and may cause you to end up with stretched ear lobes like African tribal women.

Wedding bands have caused few problems in the past but riding with a large-stoned ring is not such a good idea. With the new materials being used, the average, cheap glove is like a second skin. Rocks will show up under them and ruin the line of a nice hand on the rein. Larger rocks also seem to have the habit of turning around on your finger, making putting on gloves a longer than necessary procedure.

top tip Small pearl studs look great in the daytime, and diamonds are always a girl's best friend when riding under lights in an evening performance.

Large bracelets and big watches appearing from under your jacket sleeves detract from an overall smart appearance. A heavy gold or silver necklace might give you a few problems when worn on board – after landing over a fence you might find it around your nose! Added attachments (such as pendants, lockets, etc.) on the chain may also be very uncomfortable when buttoned up under a shirt. Pearls, lovely as they may be, are not a practical accessory – if the string breaks, it's no fun hunting for pearls in long grass.

Body piercings are not something that either of us have experience of! The obvious no-no's are piercings on the face, eyebrows, lips and nose. These are not acceptable, whether on the ground or on the horse, because they are so dangerous – the results of a horse catching an eyebrow piercing with its head are not something that we ever wish to witness again. Tummy button piercings do not mix well with higher-waisted breeches (we are told!). Piercings in any other areas are best left to those who indulge in different past-times! (Enough said, as it makes us both feel ill just thinking about it.)

● subtle evening make-up with diamond studs

Spectacles and sunglasses

Contact lenses are preferable to ride in but if you are unable to wear them, glasses fitted with sports lenses (within plastic or metal frames) will be safer. If you wear glasses it is a good idea to put them on while buying your hat to ensure they are still comfortable and fit correctly. They will also help you see the mirror and the price! Although fashions in frames change frequently, in general, a smaller rim looks better under a riding hat. Few people have seen Elton John in a riding hat.

Sunglasses, of the sports variety, can be worn

safely when riding. For those of us outside a lot, they offer protection to the eye and delicate surrounding skin. For the instructor and the examiner, however, eye contact is difficult (sometimes a good thing but unnerving for the victims!). Designer sunglasses are gorgeous but an expensive and breakable commodity around horses.

Dark glasses are rarely seen in the ring unless they are the type with sun-reactive lenses.

Perfume and aftershave

Not many years ago the use of perfumes etc. around horses was frowned upon. The only scent to be endured was the smell of the horse and what went with it! Today both men and women enjoy having a more individual fragrance. Please show a little restraint when applying it, though – you do not want to over-power your horse or any others in close proximity. And remember: a pleasing fragrance can, with time, turn old and stale and linger on your jacket – quite unpleasant.

Ladies and gents, let us not forget the deodorant at all times, please. It is worth taking a spare with you on very hot days and spraying your back as well before riding. Deodorant wipes are also a great help after riding at a show.

two | *underwear*

However wonderful your outer appearance, if your underwear is uncomfortable, your overall performance may be marred. In this chapter we will help put you on the road to finding the most suitable undergarments for riding in. Prepare to be amazed (and amused)!

The bra

We girls all know how that bra strap falling off our shoulder drives us mad. Couple that with nerves and a restless horse in a big class and we are in trouble. Taking one hand off the rein, removing a glove, undoing a shirt button and wrestling under your jacket and waistcoat at canter is not an option. (One of us has tried this in the past and not only failed to retrieve the bra strap but also ripped a favourite shirt in the process – boring to say the least.) Shrugging your shoulders will do little to recover the offending article, and may give the impression to the judge that you have a nervous tick!

The smaller-busted woman will find bra buying far easier than 'page-three' shaped ladies. Comfort in material and shape does make a hot summer day in riding gear more tolerable; and the larger ladies who experimented for us came up with some interesting ideas. Do not be under the impression that your jacket will hide all manner of sins. A thinner summer-weight jacket will unhelpfully

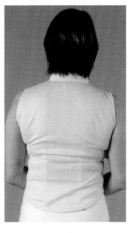

● wearing incorrect underwear can create unsightly bulges, giving the impression of a much larger image and adding as much as a dress size

● bad underwear can show, especially under a jacket that is too small

show a too-tight back bra strap, complete with underlying bulge beneath, thus ruining a neat impression from the rear.

The sports bra – a wonderful invention, or maybe not?! Most sports bras work really well as long as you are not large overall. They tend to be made in a similar way to a crop top and actually give little support. Most are constructed from a nylon-based material, which is not always the best on a long, hot day. Some now do have cotton lining, which is a great asset. The straps are designed so that they cannot fall down your shoulders. However, for the larger lady they tend to squash the breasts flat and under the armpit. This in turn can cause added discomfort, encouraging the rider to adopt chicken-wing type arms when holding the reins. Although the squashing effect prevents upward bounce, and the lady no longer looks as if she has two ferrets fighting beneath her shirt, the bounce from side to side does not go away and chafing can occur.

Our 'D'-cup-sized ladies found that correctly fitted full-cupped maximum support cotton bras were the best, especially when adapted to prevent strap loss. By sewing an extra piece of elastic across the back from strap to strap the problem is alleviated; and as

● Miss X (a 36DD) in full cotton bra, well fitted around each breast to give more control with added elastic on back and wide straps

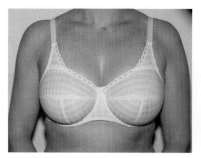

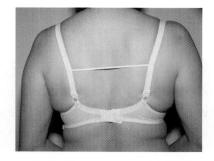

top tip To secure strap adjusters on bras, pin or sew them to prevent a southerly journey.

● this sports bra is a good example and fits well – but Miss X is more comfortable in the bra above

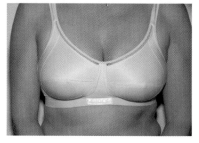

● crop-top – fun and fashionable but preferable in white

● below: spot the wrong bra

long as you are able to do up your bra from the back without problems, not at all hard to put on.

For the less well-endowed, a sports bra with cotton lining is the favourite. Teenagers found these and fashion crop tops great to wear when a vest was just too embarrassing and shirts too thin (transparent) to go around with nothing underneath.

The half-cupped bra or balcony bra is a real no-no. While wishing to attract the judge's eye, remember he needs to be focussing on your horse and not your chest. Spillage while half way round a course of jumps is most off-putting.

Likewise, wired bras are not great either, and thinking you have

● push up and pop? bra too small and padded

top tip Don't think that the bra you wear to go to work in is necessarily the right one for riding. So, if you ride straight after work, include in your change of clothes from office to stables the correct bra for the job.

top tip Never wear a front-unload bra unless you wish to unload at the wrong moment. This also applies to single hook-and-eyed secured rear bra straps. You need double hooks and eyes on any rear-fastening bra for extra width, comfort and security.

a broken rib when the wire is poking backwards under your arm is an added worry. Any bra that you would normally wear for a night out is probably going to be totally unsuitable to ride a horse in.

---

top tip Like most other garments used by a sports person, try on your 'riding' bra at home, and use it while riding before being caught out in the ring and finding that it's not up to the job.

Pants, knickers and thongs etc.

Because we spend so much time sitting on our rumps when riding, pants, knickers or boxers are often a hot topic for discussion among horse riders. (We were particularly intrigued to hear of the lady who gave herself a Brazilian wax while riding in tight, lacy French knickers under equally tight breeches. Needless to say neither of us wanted to try this one out for ourselves.) And so often we see a clear indication that the choice of underwear is unsuitable for the job required – even under full kit.

A visible panty line (VPL) at any time of day or night is something we all try to avoid. Sadly the close fit of the jodhpurs or breeches does not always make this easy. The female youth of today, wearing their tight, white, almost see-through breeches, have elected to wear thongs or strings. This is a wonderful idea as long as you go to the competition armed with a very sharp pair of scissors and a close friend or doctor to surgically remove the thong or string bit afterwards. Although hospitalisation is unreported as yet, rumour has it that more nappy rash cream is now sold than ever before since this fashion hit the horse world. Definitely not recommended by many! Certainly the diamanté versions of thongs or any pants made with a pretty bow, ribbons and lace are to be left at home in the drawer. (We have seen people wearing these, as they are so clearly visible under breeches.)

The other type of undergarment to avoid at all costs is the all-in-one body. As these garments have poppers in the gusset area you can use your own imagination as to why they are not recommended to the horse rider. They add no support anywhere and are as likely to leave you with the one thing you are trying to get rid of in the VPL stakes.

Having been party to a novice rider's knicker mistake (she wore the French lacy variety and gave herself a nasty rub that plasters and bandages could not help), it is worth remembering the following advice on how to get the sore bit to heal when you still have to ride your darling horse on a daily basis. A seat saver can help, if you can keep the blasted thing on the saddle, but the best solution for everyday riding is to do a little borrowing. Raid your male friend's underwear drawer and select some boxer shorts – the stretchy cotton variety, if possible, perhaps with a nice designer logo: go for the ones that he would choose to ride a horse in. These will be big enough to protect the area in question for the time that you are riding and the sore is healing. Sadly boxers do not fit well under tight, white breeches so you may have to think again if you are desperate to compete in the dressage or show-jumping arena. (Do remember to wash and replace the boxers in the drawer when the job is done.)

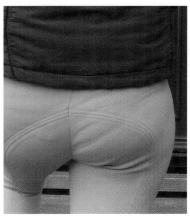

● frilly knickers, better seen fully at Wimbledon

Ladies' cotton boxer shorts are a fairly new concept. While very comfy around the stable yard, we found that they did not stay as still as they should while riding. The legs in particular seemed to roll up, especially while riding sitting trot, and readjustment was necessary. They do not seem to be cut in the same way as the gents' variety, so we suggest buying from the youths' range, and steering away from the ladies' variety. There is a problem with the leg length showing beneath the breeches, but pleated front breeches do accommodate this better.

● spots, ribbons and goodness knows what!

Please don't ever wear darker pants under lighter breeches. This is totally awful and is an unpleasant sight for fellow competitors and judges alike. There is a vast range of flesh-coloured underwear available now.

Mini, midi and tanga pants – these are not hugely comfy but better than a thong. The shape and depth

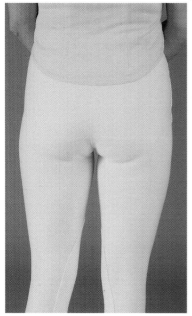
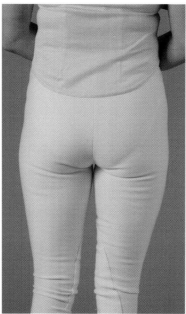
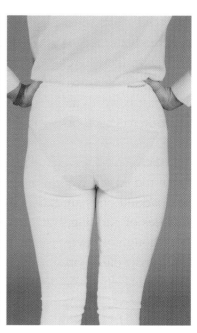

● from left to right: these pictures show the lower-legged pant, the higher leg and totally the wrong pant under very revealing breeches – clearly a case of the good, the bad and the ugly

of these designs tend to create a VPL from the start. It is almost worse than just the line of the pant legs, as it creates an indentation half way up your bum – most unattractive.

The most popular of all the tried-and-tested knickers is the good old-fashioned, high-waisted cotton pant. Not quite your Brigdet Jones look, but just as effective for comfort and ease. These are found in multi-packs in many bigger stores, so are easy and cheap to buy.

● Brigdet Jones goes riding in more flattering breeches

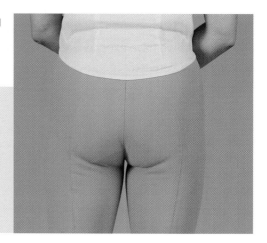

If you are a little well padded around the thigh region you are better to go for the larger, lower-legged pant. These will not leave a bulge where the pants end at the top of the thigh, an area which is very noticeable to the spectator when the rider is without a jacket. It is worth making sure that you bend your leg to a riding position to check out these lumps when having a try-on at home.

Specialist riding pants can be excellent but we found them too expensive to have enough of for use on a daily basis, and the padded ones are rather warm in the summer. There are varying degrees of padding, but we still find them too hot and unpleasant, and thought we would save wearing these for when we retire to the equestrian old people's home! If going on a marathon trek, though, we found a seat saver on the saddle more effective in preserving the nether regions.

top tip Please, please look in the mirror (a long one) at your bottom, front and back, before facing the world in your breeches or jods. You will then know if you are wearing the right undies. Bend over as you check out the rear image – any ribbing or even a slight raised pattern, albeit of the same colour but in the same material, will show up.

top tip For extra tummy control, purchase some 'magic' knickers. They really do make a difference. (Do, however, take an extra pair of normal pants to change into after riding, as we have experienced tummy trouble when wearing them all day.) If you do choose these be aware that they are often rather tight over the top of the leg. This again can create the bulge at the top of the thigh, so do try before you buy.

top tip When going to a show, remember to take a change of undies. The English weather is not always kind and shows don't stop for rain, hail or snow. Riding with wet knickers is not to be recommended.

Gentlemen's undies

There is no contest here at all. Close-fitting, stretchy cotton boxers are the only ones the boys want to wear. Beware of loose-fitting, cotton, non-elasticised boxers unless you are looking to cut short your riding career or have no intention of having children. They are definitely not a comfort option for the male rider. There is no doubt that designer names and labels get flashed about, but it is not necessary to buy these if you are watching the pennies.

Y-fronts appear totally out of fashion in and out of the horse world, with even little boys saying they were not as good as stretch boxers, due to them allowing things to escape!

 top tip
Gents, do not wear pants with stripes, colours or words on them. A lady show-jumping judge was intrigued by the rear view of a male rider sailing over a fence. The only problem was that his pants had Monday written on them, and the show was taking place on a Saturday!

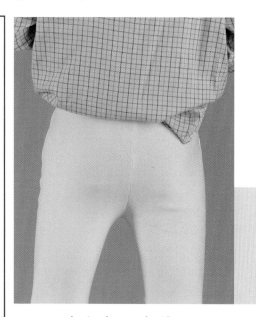

● what a bum shot!

Socks

The type and length of socks you choose is totally dependent on the length of your breeches and the tightness of your boots or half chaps. There is nothing worse than either a section of bare skin between sock and breeches, enabling that lovely bit of Velcro fastening on the breeches to eat a hole in your leg, or a very close encounter between the two, leaving you with a sock-mark for the next two days.

Most long boots are a little on the snug side so, for both males and females, a thin pop sock is a good choice. Gentlemen can, of course, invest in the smarter version and avoid embarrassment while changing footwear in public by purchasing silk socks, which have the same desired effect.

Generally speaking it is essential that you try on socks, breeches and boots at home and walk round the house in them before you leave for your competition. Remember that however well you have trained Aunt Mabel as your groom, you will have to do some walking around at the show. Showing competitors know the perils of 'uncomfortable footwear syndrome' only too well when it comes to the trot-up in hand. There is nothing more distracting for the judge than a sound horse and lame rider!

Cotton socks are another good choice and suitable for the half chap wearer and for children in jodhpurs and jodhpur boots. Again the adult rider should check the fitting of the half chaps with

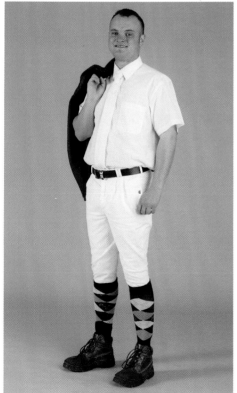

● left: fun, fitted and fine – a combination of socks and breeches made in heaven

● velcro and skin, an irritant made in hell

● ballet position number two? a thin pop sock is great inside a tight-fitting boot the length of sock chosen.

Do not be drawn into buying those new cheap socks that have no foot shape. Equally so, when you have a sock with a foot, make sure that it really does fit you. Borrowing socks that are too long in the foot will lead to the heel being half way up your ankle. This is never a comfortable option, especially if you are trying to fit a long, tight boot over the top or to do up the half chap. Likewise, too small a foot on a sock is agony when it is wrinkling under your foot.

> ***top tip*** If you choose to wear a pop sock under your long boots and the foot part of your boot feels too big or your feet are getting cold, try wearing a trainer or running-shoe liner pair of socks. These cover only the foot and do not affect the ankle or leg.

Children (and keeping them warm)

Keeping children warm, in general, is a nightmare. Keeping children warm in their riding gear is even more of a nightmare. How often have we seen the poor little things shivering on their ponies at Pony Club rallies or while standing in the ring? The advice is always the same: use many thin layers to keep them warm. A vest followed by a thin, long-sleeved t-shirt provides enough room for the shirt to fit over the top. Polo necks, however thin, are a no-go area because once the top button of the shirt is fastened and a tie is introduced, your child is likely to suffer from oxygen deficiency. Thermals or silk undergarments are a much better option. Our experience as mothers of riding children, however, has led us to believe firmly that the easy-to-find favourite T-shirt is the best option. Our kids explained how much more fun it was to have their favourite T-shirt underneath so they could still be Superman or Barbie while competing in a rather boring lead-rein class.

Tights are a great winter warmer, but please remember to buy boys the more macho thermal type to avoid them being left in the underwear drawer. (And if not already there, cut a hole in the front for easy access.) Girl's woolly tights under jodhpurs are not good against sensitive skin; the thicker lycra/cotton mix seems far more pleasing. Be sensible and go for the lighter colours for wearing under cream or beige jods. For extra warmth, add socks as well.

As mentioned before, get the children to try everything on at home first, particularly after a break from using full riding attire. Remember how the little darlings grow? Either that or try not feeding them!

● keeping warm the easy way (note how this rider has shortened her tie - no chance of it escaping from the bottom of her jacket)

> ***top tip*** If using tights and socks put the socks under the tights. This stops the socks from pulling the tights down. Knee-high socks are the best, and thermal knee-highs better still.

 **three** | # shirts, ties, waistcoats, stocks and gloves

Having sorted out your undergarments, we can now turn our attention to the items of clothing that you wear on your upper body, along with your jacket.

Shirts

People often think that a shirt is a shirt and no big deal. When combined with a neat-fitting jacket and close-fitting jods, the cut matters and comfort is essential. All shirts, whether worn with a tie or a stock, must fit well and be of a plain colour or discreet stripe or check.

Cotton is a good choice for the summer, as long as you have not developed an allergic reaction to the ironing board. A mixed fabric is a better option if this medical condition applies to you. These fabrics have been developed to provide easy-wear, stretchy garments that are breathable and therefore better on the perspiration front.

With many different styles and types there is a huge selection to choose from, but we strongly believe that the fit is of paramount importance. If a shirt collar does not fit properly, it looks tatty and very secondhand. If too big, it looks sloppy and no tie will stay in place unless stapled to your throat! Beware of your collar being too tight unless you wish to turn a shade of blue or purple. You need to establish your neck size properly by using a tape measure.

The type of collar should be considered: cut away, buttoned down or a collar of a different colour to your shirt. These will show off a well-knotted tie and look neat.

Ladies wearing men's shirts with the correct collar size will find them less restricting across the back and shoulders but often too long and wide in the body. Some men's shirt makers do accommodate lady buyers, with beautifully tailored shirts. Thankfully, it is no longer difficult to buy ladies' shirts that fit at the neck, the bust, body and arms. You may even find one in a large department store where they have a children's section. Most youths need a smaller collar size, so this can be an easy way of finding a fitted shirt. Charity shops are another potential source. We have both found some lovely striped and plain shirts in such places. There are, of course, expensive outlets for women's riding shirts, but please do

> *top tip* Try on your shirt with your breeches before you leave for a show. If it doesn't tuck in easily you will have an uncomfortable day.

● well-ironed, but clearly her husband is short of a shirt

● much neater

• just look
at the
difference

look elsewhere if money is a concern.

The shirt you wear must be a proper shirt. Ladies' blouses and girls' school shirts are often made with a rounded collar and a scooped neckline. These are totally unsuitable for wearing with a tie and sadly seen all too often at horse shows and Pony Club rallies.

Men do have an easier job. Whatever man's shop you go to, you will be sure to find the right collar size and style.

Show-jumping shirts sometimes have a detachable round collar. Again, these look very smart when the collar fits the rider's neck. A bad fit looks sloppy and can lead to the 'country-cousin' look. The

• 'dog collar' –
detachable collar
on ladies' show
jumping shirt

• too tight, wrong
sleeves, wrong
collar – don't wear it

trendier jockeys have their initials on the front of the collar, which is rather fun and stops anyone else 'borrowing' your clothing. Sponsorship names and logos have become very popular and are to be seen on shirt collars, effective from the advertising point of view and reminding us all that bills need to be paid. A detachable collar is handy for stay-away shows where washing machines are in short supply. (Remember to pack perfume as well, though, if you intend to change collars and not the shirt for more than two days.)

Soft pastel colours make a welcome change from white and look attractive on and off the horse. However, these shirts should not be worn for any other discipline, especially dressage. Gentlemen do not have this option as they are still required to wear a white shirt and tie while show jumping. This is also the only time you will see white shirts and ties worn with tweed.

Shirt sleeves also involve more choices. Long sleeves dangling out of the end of your jacket over your knuckles is not a good option. A snippet of shirt sleeve protruding from your jacket can certainly add a touch of class when correct, however. Short sleeves are useful, comfortable and still look fine when the jacket is removed. The sleeveless variety is getting very popular and can now be found in a breathable material.

Fairly new to the market is the totally fitted full-collared or stock shirt. This comes in a modern breathable material, dries in a second and requires no ironing. It is so well fitted that it has a waist, and is of such a length that you do not need to tuck it in. These shirts are a little on the pricy side but are a must for any wardrobe as they are so user-friendly, unlike the old-style hunting shirt.

● show-jumping short-sleeved shirt, with tie retaining details

● 'my arms have shrunk'

● old-style hunting shirt   ● more correctly seen in a high chair?

If wearing a stock, it is essential that you have a stock shirt that boasts a mandarin collar. Often these collars are a little big but a small dart in the back will correct this. Don't worry if you can't even thread a needle: it doesn't have to be the neatest stitching, as once the stock is tied it will hide your handiwork.

On really hot days a small crop-top will secure a false bib. These give the impression of a shirt and stock but without back and sleeves. Beware of using these bibs, as they are not very comfortable and are hard to keep secure and flat without a tin of safety pins. Both of us feel underdressed in them but there are many, particularly of the younger generation, who love them.

In our opinion it is not an option to wear a crop-top or T-shirt and then just put a stock around your neck. However well fitted your jacket, you are bound to display a bit of flesh or T-shirt, which is totally unacceptable. Your stock will also suffer, no matter how well tied, with nothing to secure it to (unless you are attempting a new form of body piercing).

Shirt ends or tails need to be of a decent length to tuck in, but

top tip

Do look in charity shops. You could be amazed at what you find for only a fraction of the price!

not so long that you have to find somewhere for reams of material. Having avoided the dreaded VPL, why stick a bundle of shirt down your breeches? If your bottom didn't look big before, it will do now! Equally so, not tucking your shirt in at all should be saved for the teenagers in the school playground. Light breeches with a dark shirt tucked inside them will create a similar shadowy effect to black knickers. Heaven forbid that your zip undoes itself while you are going around the ring, but at least if your shirt is of a similar hue and your Brigdet Jones pants are the right colour, all dignity will not be lost! Colour choice is very individual but do remember to think about your overall co-ordination. When riding horses and hacks that sport a coloured browband this is essential.

● the half Windsor knot (see tying method below)

Ties

Without a doubt you must coordinate your tie to your shirt. Loud and garish is not the order of the day. A correct tie knot (ideally a half Windsor) will ensure a neat overall appearance. Practice makes perfect, and do remember that you will need a tie pin.

● tying a half Windsor:

1. cross left (wide part of tie) over right (narrow part of tie), and back under right

2. pass wide part down through the V and across to left

3. bring wide part across the front from left to right

4. push wide part up through the V, and down through front of knot

finish by running the knot up to the collar while holding the narrow part; then tighten the knot by pulling the wide part (while holding the knot)

Wonky ties, or ties that have escaped from the front of your jacket, will totally detract from your overall appearance. It is also unsightly to see the end of the tie protruding beneath the jacket, especially if wearing a cut-away. For ladies this can be particularly embarrassing, as you may appear to have had a sex change.

Colour of tie, shirt and jacket should all go together and if you want to be really fancy, try to match to the colour of your horse. We all know greys are complemented by blue shades, but does this work as well when put with a bay horse? We think not.

● correctly knotted tie, showing a half Windsor and a correct collar

● what to wear, but how not to wear it!

● neat colour coordination

 top tip The half Windsor knot is 'the' knot to do. It does not slip, looks tidy and remains centre point to the collar. You definitely need a thinner tie to make this look really good, and even we have learned how to do it, eventually!

top tip Buy narrower ties. They are far easier to make into a small, neat knot.

top tip Cheap nylon ties tend to slip their knot and do not seem to remain up into your shirt collar. Silk ties are by far the best, so remember to have a rummage in those charity shops.

Waistcoats

Waistcoats are not essential when riding in show jumping, eventing or dressage, unless you hit the higher levels in dressage where a cutaway jacket with tails is required. The side-saddle rider will always need a waistcoat due to the nature of the cut of the habit jacket.

Waistcoats should be of a plain colour or quiet check. There are many different options when looking to buy a waistcoat but make sure that it fits you well or it will affect the hang of your jacket. Waistcoats can have a wonderful corset effect although, if too tight, taking deep breaths is not easy.

● warm waistcoat but we suggest long sleeves may be sensible for warmth and covering larger biceps

● cool!
the false
waistcoat

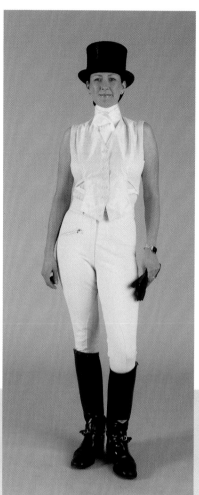

Waistcoats are made in a variety of different cloths and provide
different levels of warmth. All come with a satin-effect back, apart
from the false waistcoat which is a must for the warmer weather.

These undergarments can look very smart, especially when worn
with a cut-away jacket. Attention to length is important, as the
waistcoat should show the front points below the jacket front only in
the cut away. A lovely jacket can be totally ruined by an overstated
waistcoat, especially if the latter is too long in the front tails.
Remember to check your patterns and checks. As a general rule you
should wear a plain waistcoat with a checked tweed and perhaps be
a little more experimental with a blue or black jacket. A waistcoat
should enhance your clothing not be a statement on its own.

● too, too big – this will make her jacket bulge

>  ***top tip*** Try on all waistcoats with your own jacket on top. Odd as this may sound, you may find that the length is quite different under your own.
>
> ***top tip*** investigate the weight of the cloth. Unless you are standing around for a long time, a waistcoat can get warm to ride in.
>
> ***top tip*** Do use a false waistcoat on a hot day, with a cut-away jacket, as you will feel a huge difference in the over-heating stakes with the false back. These look smarter than the imitation waistcoat points that you can attach to your jacket.
>
> ***top tip*** Avoid pocketed waistcoats. They may make your jacket bulk out in the wrong places. However gentlemen's waistcoats always come with them – most important for the fob watch!

Stocks

top tip

Don't be a
wimp! Never
give in to the
pre-tied stock.

These really do need to be always worn with a stock shirt. The better fitting the collar, the easier the stock will be to tie. If coloured stocks are used, they must be worn only with a tweed jacket for the appropriate discipline. Event riders still favour them, but on the whole, a shirt and tie with a tweed jacket is more commonly seen. For the lady rider in the blue or black jacket in a class requiring it, a cream silk stock is a final, luxurious, finishing touch. Never will a pre-tied stock look the same. In fact, we would go so far as to say that such a horrid garment will detract from the overall turn-out.

Stocks were originally designed to protect the rider's neck from whiplash injuries. The false stock is such a poor relation – it throws tradition and etiquette out of the window.

Gentlemen may wear a silk equivalent, but are more commonly seen in the hunting stock, which is made of cotton. On the thicker male neck this can look good; for the female it takes away the impression of a long slender neck.

Tying a stock is not easy but is possible. As with all things, practice will make it easier. A short stock is impossible to manage,

right: pre-tied,
too big, too bling,
too awful

far right: an
elegant and
correctly tied stock

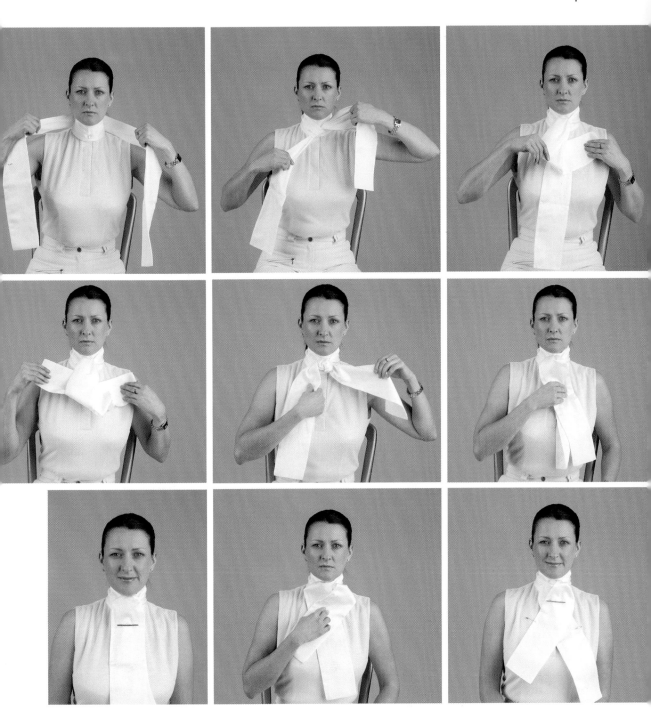

● practice makes perfect – either finish is correct,
but please make sure your pin is horizontal

and certainly the old-fashioned three-fold type are not as easy to get looking neat unless you have had some really good instruction. You must have some safety pins at the ready to secure the bottom flaps of the stock – seeing these flap over the top of your jacket is a sight for sore eyes and will lead the inexperienced spectator to think you have forgotten to remove your napkin after lunch. The sign of a true pro is seeing them tying his or her stock while on the run!

There are two suggested methods to use, both are correct and the choice is dependent on the length of your neck and the preferred style.

top tip Always wipe or wash your hands clean before handling a silk stock. Baby bum wipes are a handy addition to both car and lorry.

top tip Regarding the silk stock, do not be put off by the 'dry-clean only' label. We have always put ours in the machine on a delicate wash with no problems.

top tip Check that your stock pin copes with the combined thickness of your stock and your shirt, especially as the breathable stock shirts have a double-edged cotton button-front.

Stock pins and tie pins

When choosing a stock pin to wear on the cream or white stock, try to avoid anything too fancy, and certainly don't opt for the 'bling' look. Steer clear of the fake-gold fox-head look. Not only do these look cheap but also they tend to bend as you put them through the stock. The same will happen as the pin tip becomes blunt – in fact stock pins have a habit of cutting into your finger as you attempt to put them through the material of the stock and the shirt so it's worth remembering to pack plasters. The cheaper versions of stock pins will eventually suffer from metal fatigue, so it is worth having a spare at all times.

The stock pin and tie pin can double up as one, which sadly a lot of tie wearers seem to forget. Many, many years ago when we were both setting out on our careers with horses, a tie flapping out of your jacket and going over your shoulder was not deemed to make you either look or go as fast as the Red Baron. In fact, a fallen fence was often attributed to the horse looking back up at his rider's flapping tie! Many a time we have seen a show-jumping rider stuffing his tie back into his jacket (a bit like the slipping bra strap) yet this is so easily rectified, even if you just use a safety pin!

● the 'bling' pin is impractical to hold a stock correctly – a plain pin is more correct and will do a better job

 top tip Stock pins have a habit of disappearing. Attach yours to the lining of your jacket after removing to save endless searching before the next competition.

 top tip If using granny's heirloom or an antique present, get a safety chain and pin fitted. The original, older pins were made to go through only the finest of silk and they tend to pop undone when used on heavier modern-day materials – but, boy, do they look classy!

Gloves

Gloves should be like a second skin and are far better to ride in when they fit your hand well. Do not make life more difficult for yourself by having too much material between you and the reins. With modern materials even warm gloves do not need to be bulky. Leather gloves, once so expensive that you could only have them as a best pair, are now far more affordable. With the introduction of polyurethane synthetic gloves, you can always pretend that you are wearing the real thing. These wonderful copies can more easily be washed and do not suffer as much on a wet day, nor leave you with brown hands when the dye runs. Many of us feel

 top tip Wash your gloves while they are on your hands, and remember to wash your hands thoroughly afterwards to remove any dye stains.

clockwise from top left:

● smart, but making the hand very obvious

● a nice glove for day-to-day riding, but totally incorrect for the ring

● eat your heart out, michael schumacher

● too much flesh, darling!

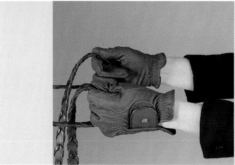
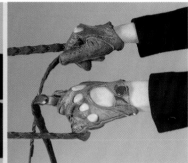

top tip

If you suffer from cold hands and still wish to wear leather or similar, purchase some silk gloves to wear underneath.

that there is nothing like the real leather glove to ride in, but it is worth trying the synthetics on days when the British weather is not at its best as they will slip less on wet reins.

Gloves nearly always look better when of a darker colour; and certainly darker gloves are a better option for most classes. Black gloves, however, should really only be seen at funerals and not on a horse. It is totally correct to wear dark brown with a black jacket, providing a nice contrast and finish to the jacket sleeve. Cream ones look classy next to a navy or black dressage jacket, as long as you are capable of riding with a still hand. On a sharp horse nobody wants to see how busy your hands are – let's face it, you don't want to look as if you are doing the washing-up!

Do make sure that the cuff of your glove is long enough. A smart, expensive glove ceases to be so when exposing a section of hand at the wrist end.

Likewise double-back fastenings at the wrist are great for daily wear but too bulky under your jacket sleeve. Woollen or pimple gloves, found in all colours, are great for long hacks, especially in the winter, but for adults and children alike are not nice enough to

a neat and tidy rider with correct everything! this outfit would be suitable for lower level affiliated dressage, for all else at riding club level, and for show jumping at a lower level with a change of hat

top tip Go into a shop and find out your correct glove size. No matter how well you ride or how easy your horse is, fitted gloves make a difference. Also knowing your size means you can add gloves to your wish-list for Christmas, making it easy for the buyer and helping to prevent wasted trips to exchange.

top tip If you are using lighter coloured gloves that need cleaning, wash them in tepid water. Always use leather-washing liquid, but if stuck without and desperate, use a good shampoo. This is much kinder to the leather and does not have such a hardening affect.

top tip If you suffer from sweaty palms sprinkle baby powder into your gloves before you put them on. This also helps when putting on new or just-washed leather gloves. Always be ready with the wet wipes after you have put on your gloves to ensure no stray powder gets on to your jacket.

top tip If your precious leather gloves get wet, stuff them with tissue or newspaper paper and dry away from direct heat. Before they are totally dry put them on and open and close your hands a few times. This helps to stop them shrinking and maintains their shape.

be seen in public. Car-driving gloves are fab in cars but looking as if you are about to take part in a Formula 1 race is not good etiquette, nor will they inspire your horse to go any faster in the jump-off.

four | *breeches and jodhpurs*

With the enormous array of jods and breeches available today, riders of every different shape, size and height should be able to find the perfect fit. It is hardly surprising, however, that people take one look at the mass of clothing on offer in a shop, and think, where do I start? It is a well-known fact that saddlery shops have a limited amount of space for display and stock, so selecting a suitable variety of breeches can be quite a challenge. If you, like us, spend most days in breeches you become aware of the different makes that are comfortable and will often stick to the same manufacturer because of this. Breeches do not have a bottom cuff at the end of your leg. They are designed to have a smooth end to the garment, enabling them to fit into your long boot with ease. The end of the leg is fastened flat with Velcro. The same principle is employed when wearing the half chap, as extra material can cause rubbing and discomfort.

Jodhpurs are designed to be worn with a short boot and normally are seen on children.

A sewn-in piece of elastic, or, for those of you unable to thread a needle, a joddy clip, can be used to attach the end of the jodhpur leg to your heel, around your boot. This stops the bottom of the jodhpurs rolling up and parting

● true jodhpur and boot

● pull-on stretch jods – not easy to wear, even for the smaller lady

company with the boot. The joddy clip attaches under the heel and onto either side of the leg by use of metal crocodile clips and strong elastic. Children, on the whole, find this impossible to do themselves. Jodhpurs provide a more finished look compared to breeches when worn off a horse without the use of a full boot or half chap. They are rarely worn by adults due to the problems they create with the long boot and the half chap.

Looking at your body shape and making sure what style will suit for comfort and appearance is your first step forward. You must be realistic about this and not ignore the extra additional body mass you may have acquired over the years. Breeches can look very

● high waisted, low waisted!

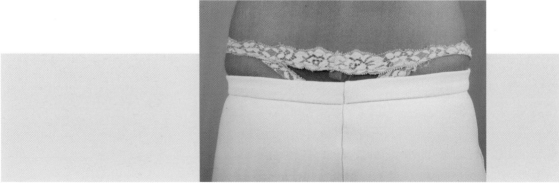

sexy, but get the fit and the shape right. Shorter-bodied people may not find the high-waisted breeches any use for obvious reasons.

You must be comfortable from the waist down, therefore take time to assess the different styles and learn which ones are right for you. It is a good idea to sit on a saddle horse while trying breeches pre-purchase. What may appear to be comfortable when standing upright can be totally different when you are bent double or in a sitting position. This is also true of the tightness around the knee.

Unless you have a washboard tummy and svelte figure, the wearing of what amounts to leggings is far from the image required, but you will find plenty of these on the market. They may be very easy to pull on and comfortable to wear, but they offer very little protection or support. After one outing with the horse they may need to enrol at the gym in the saggy, baggy class.

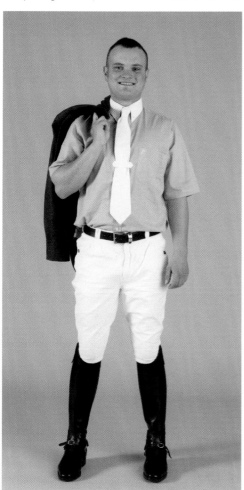

Gentlemen tend, we feel, to look far better in pleated-front breeches. The cut is suited to all figures of men – short, tall, fat or thin – and does not provide an embarrassing tight area at the groin.

Guys, please do not be seen anywhere in tight nylon jods. Not only does it look really unprofessional but also the Rudolph Nureyev look is not designed to be seen anywhere other than at the ballet!

● left: looking good, with correctly carried lunchbox

● pleated normal waist breeches, stylish and smart, shown with a good shirt and tie

All fuller-figured women who host a bit of tummy, will be better wearing a flat-fronted garment with the zip at the side. Add a pair of tummy-control knickers and you will feel much happier about your overall appearance. If you feel that your orange-peel thigh may show, there is now help at hand. The latest addition to the 'hide-it-all' clothing department are the inner-meshed breeches, which cover all dimples and bumps – hooray, no more cellulite! There are few breeches or jodhpurs designed for the larger and shorter adult female. If you are vertically challenged and over an English size 16 you will have a hard time finding the waist measurement you need with a shorter length of leg. Generally, manufacturers produce a regular and long leg. For some unknown reason they have not realised that there are some of us out here who do not have legs up to our armpits! The easiest way, and for some people the only way, of getting round this, is to get the fit right at the top and then cut off the pools of material around your feet. This is an easier operation on jodhpurs than on breeches and, of course, restricts you greatly on the material and style you want. There is no way that this is a safe procedure to conduct on leather-seated breeches or even the fake leather variety. You will also need to be aware that putting a tight boot over the top could be impossible. If this is the case, the half chap or gaiter may be the only option open to you.

A pleated front looks fantastic on smaller-tummied women and is very comfortable to wear, especially when working in the yard all day.

Side pockets can add inches to your hips, and have very little value.

top tip
When buying competition breeches, check which colour is acceptable for the class you are aiming to do.

Let's face it, when you are young and slim most things are wearable, but style and cut do cover the over-indulgences at the cake shop. Do not just look at your jods or breeches as your latest fashion accessory. They are, in effect, a sports trouser and must behave in a way suitable for your requirements and comfort. Remember also that at a competition we often get changed in a limited space. There

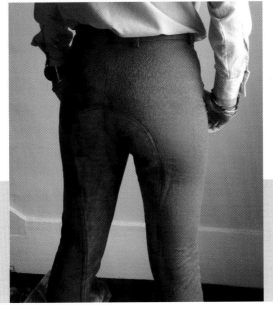

 full leather-
seated with
unusual pattern,
fantastic for not
showing the dirt,
and classy

is very little chance of finding enough room to lie on the
floor and use a coat hanger to do up your zip. This is
certainly not to be tried in the tiny portable loos seen at
most shows – they are not as robust as they appear, and
falling out of the door half zipped up is certainly not a good
start to the day.

Whenever you are on the road to making a purchase,
take with you the boots that you are going to wear. It is also
a good idea to be wearing the right undies; the wrong ones
and the overall look may be ruined through lack of
thoughtful preparation. This in turn may mar your judgement
on what you finally choose. Treat this expedition in the
same way as you would if shopping for a special outfit
for any other occasion. Make sure your underwear, socks
and boots are correct for the choice of clothing you are
trying on.

Many breeches have synthetic or leather
half or full seats which extend down the inner leg. These
will need to tuck into your boot at the point where the boot
is at its tightest at the knee. If your boots are already on the
tight side this may not be an option for you and you may

> ***top tip*** When
> buying pleated
> breeches do not squeeze
> into the tightest pair you
> can find. Once the pleats
> are pulled flat it creates the
> illusion that you are bigger
> than you are.

> ***top tip*** Never
> tumble dry your
> breeches – it's just too
> depressing! You will either
> need a coat hanger to
> winch them back on or
> have to place an
> advertisement in the paper
> for a new, smaller owner.

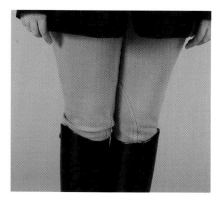

have to stick to material only. You may need to address the sock issue as well. Tight-fitting half chaps can also cause a problem, so be prepared.

The introduction of the synthetic seat has been a wonderful boon. For those of us attempting to do medium trot on a leather saddle, this extra grip can make all the difference. The fact they don't need the same care and attention in washing and drying as real leather is another bonus.

• baggy mistake! cheap and nasty pull-on equestrian leggings (such bad taste)

The cotton jods of yesteryear are now usually found to have an added ingredient of stretchy material. This aids them in keeping their shape.

When choosing everyday breeches/jods, durability and comfort is perhaps more important than style. It is worth remembering that you will be moving around much more, so tightness, especially around the waist, is not a good idea. We can all put up with that for short periods of time, say, for a competition, but not when working all day. Do, however, bear in mind that big checks will make you look even larger, as will any form of horizontal pattern or stripe. Dogtooth pattern or small checks are more user-friendly for most figures.

• super, fun and practical

With such an enormous array of colours and materials available, the first-time buyer is well advised not to shop in a hurry. The advent of brighter pastel colours has enabled the everyday rider to have a more varied wardrobe but, as with all lighter colours, these are not so great at hiding the dirt. The introduction of a darker, matching colour over the bottom and legs of some such breeches can make even the smallest derrière look bigger than necessary and should certainly be left for the younger generation to enjoy. A darker colour in this area creates an inner circle around the bottom and draws the eye to the wrong place (great for target practice).

Full-seated breeches not only protect the rider from chafing; with this addition of thicker, heavier material

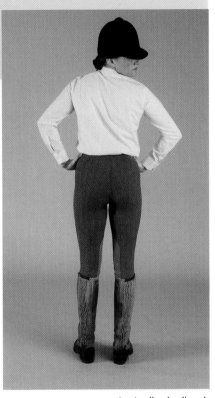

● does my bum look big in these? these pictures clearly show the difference the colour of the inset makes; note also the full-seated breeches

● yes, it does

● a little bit

● not at all, darling!

there is also less chance for the knees, seat and gusset area to wear out. Caution should be taken when buying these in the summer, as they are much hotter to work in than others without this additional panel. Most breeches will have a reinforced piece in this area, but watch out for the cheaper copies. These start off life looking respectable but regular use combined with washing sees them lose

top tip With all breeches check the quality and thickness of the material. This especially applies to the bottom gusset and knee area, which will wear first.

● how things have changed – certainly these breeches do not carry an 'easy care' label

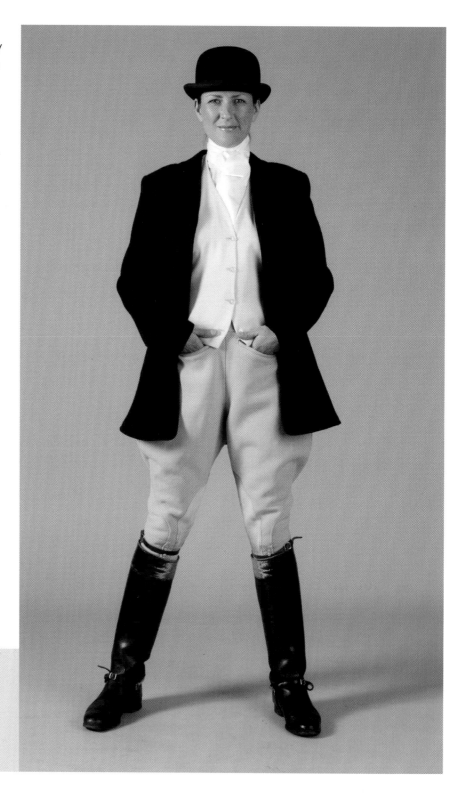

their elasticity and shape far more quickly than the budget will allow for a new pair.

Be aware that yellow or canary can make the breeches look as if they are coming along on their own first! If you have large thighs, stick to the paler colours of this hue.

• thicker material would be a little kinder

top tip With all breeches check the quality and thickness of the material. This applies especially to the bottom gusset and knee area, which will wear first.

top tip If you wish to take part in an all-round range of activities, choose a neutral beige or buff colour. In these you can never be wrong, and the bank balance is aided because you need buy only one pair of competition breeches. Canary yellow, for example, is acceptable in the show ring but not for the dressage rider. Natural beige or buff may be used in either.

top tip White is a harsh and difficult colour to wear. If you are aiming to be a dressage queen or show jumper, unless you are slim and very trim, choose a cream rather than stark white. If your choice is white, pay particular attention to the weight of the material. If thin and tight every lump, bump and hint of cellulite will show up. Your choice of underwear will have to be carefully considered as well. This is also true of the cheaper makes of beige or yellow breeches.

top tip Buy the best you can afford. Generally we have found the more expensive to last longer and wear better. Do, however, be wary of the designer labels. These may be quite a bit more than some of the others and may not be any better made.

boots, chaps and spurs

We all know that tight shoes, rubs and blisters make any day long and uncomfortable. No matter what you are doing, correctly fitting footwear is a must. No athlete would consider taking part in a track event with trainers the wrong length and width, nor would they put those trainers on for the first time on the day of the event. It therefore never ceases to amaze us how many people do just that on the day of a competition. Trying boots on, be they long or short ones, in a shop for five minutes is simply not enough time for the two of you to get to know one another.

The make of riding boot you opt for is a very individual thing, and is usually dictated by the cash you have to spend and the discipline you have chosen. This is the same for both long and short boots. This chapter should help you make a good choice first time around and avoid the expensive mistakes so many of us have made in the past.

Short boots and jodhpur boots

Not so long ago, when elephants were fish, the only short boot that was safe to ride in was the plain brown or black jodhpur boot. As this was the only boot on offer, it is hardly surprising that the older members of the horse world sport the best chilblains and bunions

● short boot worn with full chaps and spurs

you have ever seen. In those good old days, short boots were neither comfy nor warm. Some of the more trendy types attempted to ride in Doc Martins, only to discover that they had to leave their stirrups attached to their feet forever more, as the boots were so wide. Desert boots also became popular for a while but had the same problem, so were not sensible on the safety side of things. The cowboy boot also became a fashion hit, but when used with an English rather than a western saddle, they provided the rider with the worst pinched legs ever. Nowadays there is a huge range of boots varying in styles and prices. From plain to patterned, zipped to laced, with padded arches and steel toecaps, or with all of those features in one boot, you are bound to find one that attracts you.

Before selecting your style, you must decide what the purpose of the boot is. Today it is totally acceptable to ride in short boots and gaiters in most levels of competition. The fabulous designs of the gaiter can really fool anyone into thinking the rider has a full-length boot on. Matching the boot to the gaiter is essential, but don't be conned into believing that you have to buy the same make in both to achieve this. Often different gaiters fit different makes of boot, but please make sure the colour is the same.

Boots worn around the yard must be supportive, totally comfortable and, above all, safe for the jobs they have to do. With vast price differences, our advice is to go for the most comfortable you can afford. There is no doubt that the very cheap boot does not always do the job or last long enough. The shape of the foot is important if your feet are to remain happy through the day, and the overall look and fit of the foot in the stirrup is important. Extra-thick soles may last longer but for the competition rider look bulky and unattractive. Laced boots do look fab, but remember how long they take to get on and off.

---

 top tip When trying boots in a shop, walk round a lot with the boots fully fastened to see if they rub your ankles or feet.

 top tip While wearing the boot in the shop, bend your knees to adopt a lower leg riding position. You will then see if the boot has enough 'give' at the ankle to allow you to do huge kicks if required.

 top tip If buying in summer for everyday use do wear thick socks – you will need them when it's minus three degrees. If the boots are then too big in summer, add insoles to pad out. (Odour-eaters are recommended when dealing with boots belonging to teenage boys.)

 top tip Although buckles and pop studs on the top of boots can look great, they don't feel great when sticking into your ankle secured by a half chap.

Half chaps and gaiters

What a wonderful re-invention. They have actually been around for years and were collectively known as gaiters. Made of hard leather, and with laces running from the foot to the top of the leg (before the invention of the zip), they probably took a while to get into. They were worn with garter straps and are best shown in the original versions of **Black Beauty** or **National Velvet**! These extra 'legs', as we call them, are a great way of looking good on the ground and in the saddle. They are easy to wear, once you have mastered getting them on, and easy to clean. The half chap comes in suede or leather. The gaiter is made of leather and generally has a higher shaped top. (For ease of writing we have referred to both types as the half chap for most of this section.)

Half chaps come in all different styles, shapes, sizes and materials. For everyday, the suede designs are super, but do not

● full-length leather gaiter, well used and well polished but needs to match the colour of the boot better

top tip

To keep leather gaiters looking as good as a top boot, clean them in the same way with proper polish.

resemble the overall look of the full boot. The suede option is soft and pliable, therefore not having the high cut look of its leather brother. Imitation leather/suede versions are also about, and these are fully washable and a lighter weight for the summer.

● far left: suede chaps that are too short

● left: correct length of suede chap

● out of africa?

Fringes on adult half chaps are so 'last year, darling', but for children are as popular as ever. Never before have kids had so much fun dressing to ride. From zebra to tiger print, purple and pink – you name it and you can buy it in a half chap.

Is there a down side, I hear you ask? No matter what the half chaps are made of, getting them on is not so easy when they are new. They have to be oh-so-tight on the day of purchase that a winch may be required to get you into them and at least two firemen to extract you. They will be a calf size smaller than you would normally wear. Generally, they are made with the zips either on the outside of the leg or up the back of the leg. Depending on the make, the zip may do up from the top or from the bottom. Those of you out there with back problems, beware. Tackling a zip running from the heel to the knee on the back of your leg requires the suppleness of an Olympic gymnast! So far, the easiest method we have found is to put your leg up onto a rail as high as you can, then, without losing your balance, bend sideways and start zipping – not good for the back or hangovers. Sadly this type of chap can also cause other health problems. As they slacken off in tightness with wear, they become incredibly easy to undo. Unfortunately that means they sometimes come undone while you are riding along – and if you think it's hard to do them up while on the floor, try doing it on half a ton of moving horse.

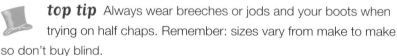

 top tip Always wear breeches or jods and your boots when trying on half chaps. Remember: sizes vary from make to make so don't buy blind.

 top tip Use a hard dandy brush to clean mud and grease from suede half chaps.

top tip For ordinary riding, clean the leather gaiter as you would your tack, with water and saddle soap.

The side zips are much easier in all ways and do not need such dexterity. However, the side-zip chap, no matter what material, will never pass itself off as a pretend full boot.

 top tip All half chaps and gaiters are much easier to clean when on your legs – but not while wearing your best breeches!

top tip This tip is definitely not in the manufacturer's guide of care. If you find that your chaps are becoming very baggy, pop them in the washing machine and run them through a cool wash with no detergent (unless you have leather-washing liquid), and dry them away from direct heat. This will tighten everything up. As yet we have not ruined a pair doing it. We do not, however, suggest you do this unless the chap is otherwise unwearable.

The full chap

Not long ago these were the only type of over-trouser available. Both of us have had our leather versions for years. The more you wear them, the better they look and feel. When buying it is worth remembering that these should last you a very long time, so take advice on the fit. The Americans have the greatest variety of colours and designs and will even stamp your initials on the back of the waistband (which is great for tucking the mobile phone into). In our opinion no one makes full chaps like the USA but it is a long way to go for a fitting, and unless you are experienced in that area it can be rather risky to buy mail order. The leather full chap seems to last longer than the suede equivalent. The split skin version of suede outside and leather inside is a great working chap. One of our 'men indoors' had a pair made to measure in 1982. He has only had to have one zip replaced up until now. The chaps are the same size and shape as when he purchased them (sadly he isn't!). Certainly the suede seems to stretch and starts to go baggy at the leg. The leather or split skin also does a far better job of repelling rain. For those who are brave, young and foolhardy there is always the

● smart
workmanlike rider
in leather full chaps

option, on a hot day, of riding in shorts under your full chaps. This is the American way and allows the rider to exercise the horse and then just remove the chaps to top up the tan while sipping a cold beer by the pool. The English version is to ride in jeans or fitted trousers and full chaps. This enables you to whip the chaps off before dashing to Tescos or doing the school run. None of our children has ever been impressed with us standing outside the school gates in breeches. Nowadays full chaps can also be bought in rain-resistant fabric, as well as fleece-lined to provide extra warmth.

Long boots

For the youngsters of today this is singularly the most expensive item of clothing that parents will buy in connection with their offspring's riding career. Not that long ago one of us retired a pair of boots after twenty-two years, and it is not uncommon to hear of boots being passed from generation to generation.

It is therefore essential that you do your homework and shop around. Generally speaking, the price of the long boot is now more attractive to people than ever before, and there is a wide range available off the peg. Bespoke boots may seem to cost an arm and a leg, but will probably outlast the owner. In our opinion it is hard to try out boots just by walking around the shop in them. They are not, and probably never will be, the most comfortable thing to walk about in until well worn. It is critical that you have the use of a proper saddle horse so that you can get some idea of sitting astride with the boots on. This not only tests the movement available in your ankle but

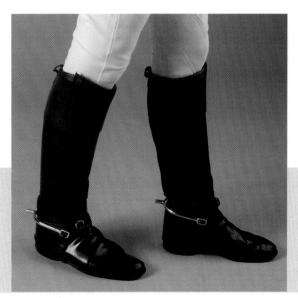

also allows you to feel the tightness of the boot. The boot must be high enough at the top of the leg to remain looking smart but not so high that it interferes with you bending your knee. This can also create a problem with mounting. Remember that the dressage boot when worn with the longer stirrup does not necessitate a much bended knee whereas the jumping rider needs more room.

The comfort factor is highly important in your choice of boot, as

● a lucky pair of hand-me-down gentleman's boots with mahogany tops; the previous owner may have been a little shorter in the leg! they should be worn with white garter straps

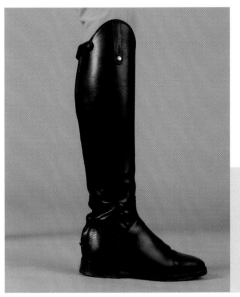

● ladies' all-round boot, showing zip at back, shaped top and soft flexible ankle; this boot is a nearly-but-not-quite as it is a little short

● although these boots are correct with the garter strap they are really too short – once on the horse they will look even shorter

is the awareness of the discipline in the sport that the boot is to be used for.

Wearing your long boots, after purchase, should not be restricted to show days. If they are your first long boots they will feel very different to ride in than a half chap. It is terribly important that you ride in them at home and in your lessons and wear them around a bit on the flat as well. Although not ever intended as a walking boot, remember they will be on your feet for a long time during a day at a show. Show riders must also be able to run in them when trotting the horse up in hand. Water-skiing behind is not an option.

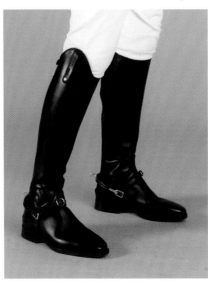

● these long zipped boots are the correct length and fit for this male rider; note the high side, back zip and ankle detail

With the invention of zips in the long boot, getting in and out is so much easier and no longer necessitates leaping off a high surface into them when you have gained a few pounds.

If you do have pull-on boots, always put them on using boot pulls. This protects the boot and (for the ladies) protects the fingernails and the boots from being scratched. If correctly fitted you may find it very hard to get them on without these special hooks. There are front and rear zips available but beware of tightness if choosing a rear unload system, as they can unload you in the middle of a dressage test. Contrary to popular belief, we can all find that our ankles get thicker after Christmas; this also applies in hot weather, so be realistic in how tight you go as there will be only be so much give when worn in.

Baggy, ill-fitting, too-low-cut boots look awful. A bad purchase on the fitting side will not cost you less than a well-fitted pair of boots.

Well-fitted boots can really improve the overall look of the rider and can even give you the appearance of the longer leg you have always wanted.

● what else can you get down there?

Do remember to be aware of the discipline that you are going to use

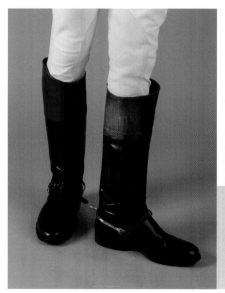

● a great pair of boots showing anything but correct fit, being too short and baggy; also the spurs are too low and the spur straps are the wrong way round

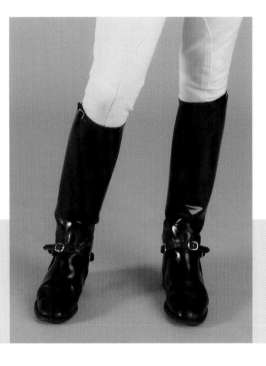

● a neat,
correct-fitting
ladies' boot,
especially
suitable for
showing

them for. Paddock boots, with the laces up the front, are more commonly seen in the jumping and eventing scene. Zipped boots with high outside knees are suited to dressage queens, male and female, and the correct footwear for the showing rider is the level-topped boot with garter straps.

● skewbald leg
to go with
skewbald horse

top tip If, at a show, you have forgotten your boot pulls and are having a quick panic attack as to how you are going to get into your boots, run to the nearest saddler's trade stand. Hoof picks make a great substitute and are cheap to buy. You may even find two in your own grooming box, and if you don't and are short of time, your neighbour in the box next door will probably be able to lend you one.

Brown boots were always traditionally worn with a ratcatcher or tweed coat. Nowadays they are not so commonly seen. They have, however, become popular with riders of coloured horses. Certainly, in among a lot of horses they can help you shine out against the rest of the crowd. Do remember that you must have

● correct turn-out for many a showing class, including a much-loved pair of waxed-calf hunting boots

brown spur straps and brown garter straps to be correct.

All said and done, you will see a variety of all these boots no matter what discipline you are watching. As long as the boot fits and is clean, the rules are far more relaxed in general than they used to be.

top tip Always wear your competition breeches when trying on boots. If tightly fitted, the boots may not accommodate full or half leather-seated breeches. The extra thickness in the panels over the knee may not go into your boots easily.

top tip Try on loads and loads of different styles. There is now a big choice on the market with styles that allow movement across the ankle, are high cut over the outside of the knee, or have zips front or back or laces at the front. Wear them all before you spend your money – they should last years and years and are a great incentive for not putting on weight.

top tip Test out your spurs and spur straps as neater ankles in long boots may require shorter spur straps. If your spur is too wide push the branches together gently.

top tip If your feet are hot or you have found that you are starting to grow out of your boots and they are hard to pull on, reach for the baby powder. Sprinkle a little into the foot of the boot and a little down the legs either side to create a more slippery surface.

top tip When at a competition, don't forget to take your boot jack or a friend who can bend over to pull off your boots. Using a step does work but can damage the back of the boot.

top tip Ladies and gents, may we suggest that you do not sit with your legs crossed when wearing your best boots? This will result in the transfer of boot polish onto the opposite knee.

Garters

The garter strap is the narrow leather addition seen attached to the flat-topped boot. Originally all breeches had small buttons on the front of the knee, which fastened to make a tight fit. Nowadays you have to sew on these buttons yourself. The garter strap lies between the second and third button. Gentlemen wearing correct hunting attire will have white garter straps against their white breeches. This is not only seen during the winter months but is also the correct dress for many championship-showing classes. A correctly fitted garter strap, both in height and tightness, will aid in the optical illusion of giving you a longer leg.

Half chaps are not made with a garter strap, although there is news that they are making a come-back, like the original old-fashioned gaiters seen in old movies.

 top tip Sew your garter strap to the back of the loop on your boot. This will prevent you having to ride with the buckle between your knees and saddle if it should slip.

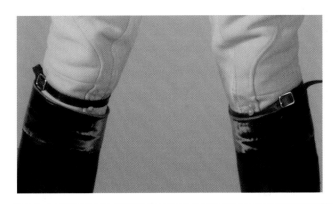

● these wonderful old breeches show the button detail – you had to allow an hour to put them on

top tip Do not be tempted to ease your boot on by pulling the garter strap as well. The loop that attaches them to the boot is unlikely to withstand such punishment.

top tip If your garter strap needs polishing refrain from using boot polish unless you wish to have it end up on your breeches. Buy some liquid polish and make sure it is dry before replacing the straps on the boot. Before putting on the boot, wipe the garter strap with a cloth just to make sure. The same method can be used with tennis shoe whitener if you are a gentleman using white garter straps.

Spurs

Contrary to popular belief, spurs are not simply worn to make the horse go faster or jump higher. They are correct dress for all adult showing classes and higher level dressage. Parents will need to check where and when their children are allowed to wear spurs, and this varies from each discipline and society. The important thing is to have your spur correctly fitted. Spurs should follow the seam of the boot and sit at the top of the heel near to the ankle bone. This is harder to get right now that many boots are made without a back seam. Most back-zipped boots do not have this seam and an incorrect spur is often seen.

● correctly fitted spurs   ● spurs fitted a little too low

The type of spur you use must suit your horse, your riding ability and the discipline you have chosen. The spur is a must in all adult showing classes but with a sensitive horse you may be well advised to wear a dummy spur. This keeps your turn-out

● boots showing medium-length shank spur set a little low and a dummy spur correctly fitted

● dummy spur showing neatly cut-off spur strap

correct and may prevent the turbo charge from coming in when not needed.

Spur straps must be the same colour as your boots and made of leather. Please leave the webbing variety for home use. Spurs should be well polished and strap buckles shiny.

 top tip If your spur is too wide for your boot, press the spur gently together to reduce the size.

 top tip Cut off the spare end to your spur strap to a neat 'V' about an inch from the buckle; this avoids any flappy bits. Blacken the cut end of the spur strap with boot polish to neaten the cut look.

top tip The buckle must be pulled as close as possible to the outside of the spur. This will ensure that the buckle remains on the outside of the boot.

top tip A spur worn too low is incorrect and ineffective; if too high you and your ankle bone will be agony.

● the only attractive thing here is the colour of the whip – we are not into rubber and whips!

PS: Rubber long boots We can only find one word for these, UCK! Anyway, who wants to ride in an anorexic welly?

six | *jackets*

Your jacket is your final top layer, so can make or break your overall appearance. Far too often the jackets we see out and about are not a good fit, and lack that essential tailored look. Today, there is no need to have a jacket specially made for you unless you have a very unusual shape or have the money to do so. There is a wide variety of jackets available with different patterns, colours and weights of cloth. But it isn't necessary to buy an endless supply of jackets: a tweed jacket and a black or navy one will suffice, no matter what level of party you are attending.

● jacketwise, you can't get much better than this

all too tight – she can't even get the shirt to tuck in!

nearly hiding it all!

There are, of course, exceptions to these generalisations but they apply to higher-ranking dressage riders and to the top end of the showing world. In these cases the dressage rider will need to wear a tailcoat in Advanced Medium classes and above, as does the advanced event rider during the dressage phase of an upper level horse trial. For the showing rider an evening performance or championship class will necessitate a change from tweed to black or navy. This is not the case for hack riders who will start in black or navy but change to stock and top hat. Gentlemen at this time will be seen in either a cut-away black or scarlet hunting coat. Ladies should never been seen in a scarlet coat in the UK, although with the sponsored jackets worn by the show jumpers, etiquette appears to have taken a sideways step. The gentleman's hunting coat should be made of pure wool, which is thick and heavy to wear. Designed to repel snow and rain and the worst blackthorns in the country, they are not always ideal on a hot day.

The heaviest is the cavalry twill at 32 ounces, which,

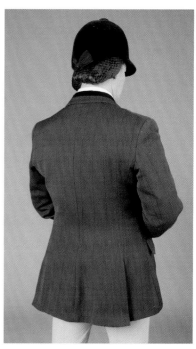

what a difference! a better cut and cloth to suit

● this blonde lady thought she was getting it right, but see how she gets a revamp on the facing page.

once wet, will hold its shape and keep you dry on the inside. The weight at this time, however, does require you to be a body builder to stand up in it! The dressage tailcoat tends to be made in pure wool of 18 ounces; this holds the shape well and falls correctly. The more modern materials, used to make them lightweight and easy care, are a poor substitute. The colour is never quite true and the material often appears to have a shine to it. The new lightweight cloth is a bonus on a summer's day but won't hang or sit correctly. In this case there is no substitute for the real thing. This can also be said of the cheaper ladies' navy or black jacket. No matter how well tailored, a shiny hue to the fabric and the lightness of it does not always provide that 'wow' effect. Quality is something that you just cannot re-create in a jacket made of a lesser material. These jackets also do little to rid any rider of the bulge factor.

Sadly, especially if they carry any stretch in them, they show every lump and bump. The lighter cotton-mixed show-jumping jackets seem to be made to a higher standard now and hang much better than some of the polyester mixes.

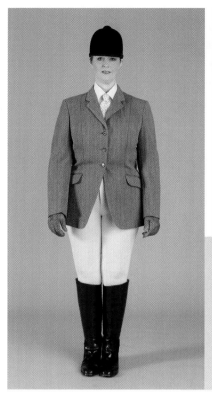

● this is a serious make-over! from mrs boring blue to confident beauty – it is worth noting that the difference in cost between the outfits shown here and opposite is minimal, barring the hunting cap.

Tweed jackets

There is now a huge choice of jackets of this type on the market. Before deciding which cloth appeals to you, have a really good look in the mirror. The fuller figure will not benefit from wearing loud or large checks, and you are in danger of enhancing something that you would rather not draw attention to.

Your choice of cloth should also be made with your horse's colour in mind. Blue tweed is often hard to wear on anything but a grey horse and does few favours for the rider, contrary to popular belief. Not all fair women can carry this colour without wearing serious foundation or the use of clever accessories, either on or off a horse. It is not true that all blondes should wear blue eye shadow or blue jackets; but if they experiment with colour it is true that they have more fun!

The darker, more traditional brown checks are now seen with the addition of green, red and even orange mixed into the weave. Your body shape will not only determine the check or weave but

● different sizes, different shapes, different stories

will also dictate the cut and design you choose. Keep this in mind as you try on jackets. If you are short in the leg, a longer jacket coming down over your thigh will only make the leg look shorter. The correct length also applies when the question 'does my bum look big in this?' arises. Of course, it does look bigger if the jacket is cut too short and does not cover it. The double vent on the back of the jacket is generally a more flattering option, but this is again dependent on your bottom size, and the larger lady may find the single vent, which is more traditional, easier to wear.

Assess whether you have a short or long waist. The shorter you are in the waist, the shorter the cut of your jacket must be. For gentlemen, fitting the jacket is no easier, and again body shape must be taken into account. The Mr Pickwicks of this world are far better catered for now, with high-waisted jackets available off the peg. This allows more room and therefore comfort, and covers up that expensively created paunch very nicely. If you are a very tall man and slender with it, can we have your telephone number? If not, it is worth buying a bigger jacket and having the waist reduced. This will ensure that the shoulders and sleeve length are appropriate for your size.

This is also worth remembering when selecting a jacket for the ever-growing teenager. Male youths, in particular, seem to go through a difficult-to-fit, lanky stage. All too often the length of arm

top tip

Think about the use of a velvet collar on your tweed. If subtle, it can add just a bit of interest to your turn-out.

and shoulder width dictates a larger size. The result of wearing such a garment then makes the poor youngster look as if a coat hanger has been left in the jacket. A clever bit of alteration on the waist will help immensely, and also allow for 'letting out' when the body shape becomes more uniform. Taller teenage girls can also have this problem, and we hate to see a good jacket ruined because the waist is too large. If this is the case, the wearing of a competition number is an added problem because the string or elastic pulls the jacket in, resulting in a puckered waistline. A quick visit to a dressmaker will solve these problems and does not cost a fortune.

top tip If when buying any jacket you are between sizes, always go for the larger one. It is not very expensive to have a jacket taken in or slightly altered, and you may not lose those few pounds that you want to. If you do, you can always go smaller again.

● the typical tall, no-shape teenager – clockwise from top left: scruffy ill-fitting jacket and chaps, with red-sock-in-the-wash jods; jacket too big; and then correct and shape beginning to appear

● jacket pulled in at waist as too big and too long over back of saddle; this lovely jacket shows a double vent and will look great when grown into or altered

● below: smart chappy in a traditional tweed jacket, suitably attired for show jumping

● this second jacket shows a better fit and a single vent (note the more professional-looking, trimmed rider number)

There is no reason for male riders not to colour coordinate as well as the ladies. Shirts and ties should match with the jackets, and generally it is best to avoid using those redundant kipper ties in your wardrobe. We always think that a good tweed jacket looks far smarter on any man than a badly weighted black jacket, no matter what shape the body underneath is.

Whatever you pick, do not choose a jacket that does not hang straight and neatly at the back. Take with you your own hand-held mirror. Take a friend along as well, but one who will be honest with you. (Avoid bribing them with an offer of lunch afterwards to tell you how gorgeous you look.) Few riding clothes shops have a double mirror, so it is impossible to see both front and back at the same time.

It amazes us that this is the case with saddlery shops. Where else would you buy clothing and not be able to see what you are getting from every angle? With your small mirror you will be able to check your back view as well. With this still in mind, ask to sit on a

top tip

Teenagers may need a size that accommodates their length of arm and shoulder size. A little alteration to the waist will improve the look dramatically.

● truly fabulous . . .

● nearly but not quite . . .

● not a hope, darling

saddle horse with the jacket on. The jacket should be long enough to cover your posterior but not so long that as you rise and sit you catch it under your bum. This is also a good time to check the cut of the jacket across your thigh. Keep thinking of your own body shape, not the shape you would like to be, and consider the length with regard to bottom covering but not thigh shortening. Simulate also a jumping position. It is great to have a well-fitted jacket, but remember you need to be able to move in it, and the freedom allowed across the shoulders and back is an important feature. Do put your arms up and forward – there is no need to adopt a high-board diving stance – but you will need to be able to move about if your aim is to jump comfortably. You will also need to check the length of the sleeves. Don't forget that your arm is bent at the elbow when riding, so lift your arms to riding position. Sleeves that may have appeared too long could now be the perfect length.

One of the better-known ratcatcher or tweed jackets is 'keepers tweed'. Seen in greenish-grey or browns it is of a traditional weight and cut and suits most figures. Top on the list also is the Harris tweed, which again is a smart choice. Pure new wool seems to be the order of the day and, coupled with a fine weave, the quality and neatness is way above anything else.

Thicker herringbone tweed is our least favourite. It appears to lack the quality of the finer weaves and does not hang so well. It is also often seen to go bobbly or to pull threads due to the nature of the weave itself being so wide.

● this stylish and traditional jacket could be worn with with a topper or a normal hat

Navy and black jackets

If you wish to be totally correct, a black jacket on a lady should only ever be seen in the hunting field. Black is a difficult colour to wear. If it is your choice then consider the option of matching it with cream rather than stark white.

Many of the more modern jackets are introducing lighter coloured piping around the collar and pockets. This does at least break up that solid look but is totally unsuitable for the show ring. It appears that the fancier, non-traditional styles and colours are associated not only with the show-jumping ring, as they are now creeping into other disciplines.

These jackets are lighter in weight and generally include some stretchy fabric. As said before, they look wonderful on thinner people but leave nothing to the imagination when strained over a fuller figure.

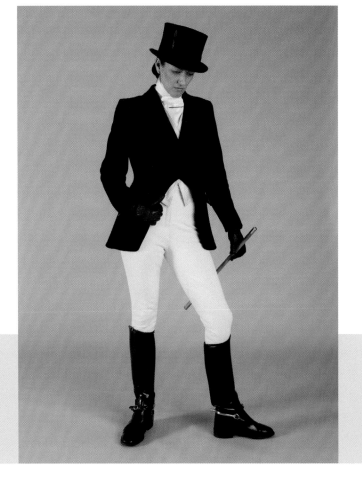

● the cut-away, looking lovely here (not suitable for larger ladies without reinforced magic knickers!)

Much the same can be said about the navy jacket but, again, as with any jacket, quality is important. The modern fabrics are easier to wear from the heat point of view, and some even save on dry cleaning as they are washing-machine friendly. They also give the show-jumping rider greater ease of movement. If you choose such a jacket, do make sure you that you are not wearing a size too small. They are less forgiving, even if you are of a smaller size, and may

> *top tip* If you find that you have suddenly grown out of your jacket, move the buttons over. This can also work if you just move the waist button or middle button a tiny bit.

● quite tasty and very smart for show jumping – a good fit all round!

🎩 ***top tip*** To improve the jacket you have, make sure it is cleaned as often as needed. Look after it by using a hanger and a clothes brush, not a nail on the back door and a dandy brush.

🎩 ***top tip*** Bright buttons do not suit all disciplines. They are fine in dressage and show jumping but not readily acceptable in other classes.

🎩 ***top tip*** Think long and hard about your whole colour scheme before purchasing a tweed jacket. This should definitely include the colour of your horse.

> **top tip** To improve any jacket old or new, change the buttons. Classy dark buttons, possibly with a fox head detail, can enhance any jacket. Don't forget to change the buttons on the cuffs as well and keep a spare sewn into the inside of the jacket in case of emergencies.

> **top tip** If you have a lightweight jacket that opens and moves as you ride round, sew some curtain weights around the bottom of the lining to ensure less tummy and bottom exposure.

> **top tip** The length of the lapel of the jacket is important. To help you look taller in the saddle, choose a jacket with longer lapels – very useful for the vertically challenged. For the larger-breasted woman, the lapels should be smaller to avoid gaping and escaping!

● nearly but not quite – lovely outfit sadly misses out on the totally correct category because of the coloured stock

● different checks – note the full and half velvet collar and the V shape created by the lapel sizes; the left outfit creates an illusion of more length in the body, while the right-hand jacket fits better

display some bits you would rather the world and his wife did not see. In general for the showing world, which still remains steeped in tradition, a fine, pure wool jacket will look better than its lightweight relation.

traditional ladies' navy wool jacket – note the double vent with a shorter section in the middle of the back, preventing the jacket from catching on the back of the saddle

Buttonholes

These should never be seen with a tweed jacket. At all costs, if you choose to wear a buttonhole for a show, it should be discreet and a finishing touch. It should never be a huge statement on your lapel. Many children in show classes appear to be wearing a huge part of their fancy browbands on their jacket lapels, matched with bows, scrunchies or ties – and the pony disappears into a sea of colour. Are the kids or the mums getting a little OTT? A small cornflower will certainly add a touch of class, but remember you are not exhibiting at Chelsea Flower Show. It is, of course, totally acceptable to wear a poppy around Remembrance Sunday. Badges, even at the risk of upsetting some societies, in our opinion, should be left in the drawer at home.

seven | *hats*

'**f you want to get ahead, get a hat'** – and by that we mean, make sure that you have the right hat for the job. Whatever hat you choose, buy it from new and make sure it has the necessary safety specifications and a British safety kite-mark. Buy it from a recommended retailer and have it fitted by a trained and suitably qualified person. We all know that riding is a risk sport, and while it is impossible to protect every part of your body, a suit of armour is not easy to jump in. Keeping your head safe is an easier option. It simply is not good enough to stick any old hat on your head while riding. It is also a really bad idea that when your elder daughter jumps off her mount and runs to the loo, you stick little Sophie on the pony with no hat on at all.

Societies and shows have enough problems with risk assessment and insurance these days, so make totally sure that you are aware of their rules before you get eliminated for wearing the wrong hat.

There are three types of riding hat seen in showing, dressage and side-saddle classes that do not have any safety features attached to them at all. In fact the best way you can ensure that they stay on your head is to have a piece of elastic fitted to pop under your chin or behind your hair to stop them flying off at the gallop! Joking apart, the three hats in question are the hunting cap, the bowler and the top hat. All of these will stay on in a high wind if correctly fitted, but they will not save your head from a serious injury if you have a fall.

There are now no classes in Great Britain that will allow you to wear one of these hats when jumping. International show-jumping classes held in the UK have to permit it, as foreign riders do not have the same rules applied to them in their home countries. Interestingly enough, most British riders jump in these classes with their safety hats on, overcoming the enormous controversy that safety hats were the ugliest things around when they first came out.

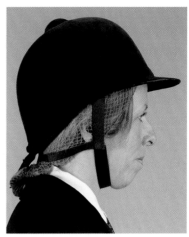

● this style is now deemed to be old-fashioned; the hat is tilted too far back on the head

Most modern safety hats carry similar safety features. Do try on different styles before you buy. The weight of the hats will differ, depending on the materials used, as will individual shapes. Go for comfort and overall appearance. A lot of three-point strapped hats seem to have been designed for someone with a wide face and a head the shape of a bucket. The riding hat in general is not the most glamorous piece of headgear but with a few trying-on sessions in front of a mirror you should manage to find something that doesn't make everyone fall about laughing when you first wear it.

As said before, the correct fit is of ultimate importance – it should be snug but not so tight that you will reaching for painkillers within an hour of wearing it. How many times have you seen someone with a huge indentation stamped on their forehead after removing their hat? The brim of your hat should always be worn horizontal to the ground, assuming you are still standing or on your horse the right way up!

There are new styles coming out all the time, usually trying to improve the comfort, safety and wearability of the hat. The ubiquitous air-vented helmet, similar to those seen on the Tour de France circuit in previous years, has now seemingly been welcomed into the horse world. We think it takes more than this particular style to keep a cool head! They are, however, a good seller we have been assured, and are used a lot by long-distance riders and happy hackers. They are very light and airy, helped by the numerous air vents, which makes them ideal for summer riding. They look very different to most other riding hats and will not appear on the traditionalist's Christmas list.

do I look cool in this? whether riding a bike or getting on a horse, these air-vented helmets are now a popular choice

The hunting cap

In days gone by, this was the hat that you had made for you, and that option is still open. If that is your choice you should never need to buy another, as you can always have it refurbished if it gets tatty. If pennies are tight there are cheaper copies available, although not bespoke. This hat comes in blue or black velvet and without any straps. If you ever see a faded one it's probably a well-worn old favourite. With a deep crown, a small peak and a fit like no other, this hat is likely to become a close personal friend. You can now have a bespoke hat made to the same specifications but with a

tweed finish, a slant on the traditional style but which can be quite fetching. When doing flat showing classes or affiliated dressage, there is no doubt that most ladies really do look totally gorgeous in them. (Some men don't look so bad in them either!)

To say that this hat is your crowning glory is no mistake. Sadly they offer little to no protection compared to the safety hat.

smart, and we like him!

top tip To avoid the crushed-velvet look store your hat in a box or away from other hats or garments.

 top tip Never store your hat in a plastic bag because velvet is not a fan of this!

 top tip Steam-clean your hat with a kettle to restore the velvet sheen or, better still, take it to the bathroom with you (but we advise removal before bathing) as velvet hats also like steam from hot showers and baths.

 top tip Traditionally, riding hats have ribbon tails, but these should be sewn up into the hat or tucked up when riding.

● this lovely shaped hat, which compliments the rider's face, giving a very smart appearance, sadly is marred by the dangling ribbons

The bowler

Gentlemen show riders and officials, in general, use the bowler hat. Ladies in side-saddle classes held before midday at county shows, will also wear them. In our experience there are few ladies who do

● right: we still like him!

● far right: this is Laurel and Hardy's bad day!

themselves any favours, as far as the beauty stakes are concerned, while in this hat.

At least the lady side-saddle rider can make use of a veil which, when correctly fitted, gives the effect of a mild face-lift, always a bonus. There is no doubt that a correctly fitted and shaped bowler makes the difference between a comedy turn and a professionally dressed rider.

 top tip As bowlers are expensive to buy, it is worth checking out antique and bric-a-brac shops or car boot sales. The Side Saddle Association also has a list of places where hats are for sale and for hire, especially for the ladies.

 top tip Check the shape of the bowler's brim. If it's too wide and flat you will resemble Laurel and Hardy on a bad day.

top tip If buying a secondhand bowler and it is a little too big, add draught excluder to the inside rim. This comes in a self-adhesive roll and is just the right width to make your hat a better fit.

top tip You may only wear a bowler hat with a shirt and tie, never with a cream or white stock, except while hunting

● this lady is the exception to the rule when it comes to wearing bowlers – she looks fantastic; shown in traditional hunting style

Top Hats

The top hat is a highly flattering piece of headgear, whether worn by males or females. The art is to get the correct height and width to suit the shape of your face and your frame. Herein lies the difference between you looking quite gorgeous or like someone off to the mad hatter's tea party! If you can afford it, a bespoke, hand-made top hat will last forever.

Ladies' older silk top hats are hard to find, especially if they have any history to them. They are shorter in height, not exceeding 4.5 inches, which eliminates the chance of you looking as if you have a chimney pot on your head. The difference between the show rider's top hat and the dressage rider's top hat is the shape of the brim and the

● although on a beautiful woman, this hat is too tall

● a nearly-but-not-quite correctly fitted and shaped dressage topper, just a little tall (spot the horrid stock and bling!)

• a correct-sized top hat showing elegance and charm

material and height. The dressage hat is generally shorter and made of felt. The show hat is made of silk. This is why you see such a beautiful sheen on top hats worn under lights in evening show classes.

Again, toppers are not always easy to find, but the same rules can be applied as when looking for a bowler.

The top hat is traditionally used in evening performances and championship classes, and is always worn with a silk stock by ladies and a hunting stock by men. On the elegance side we think there is nothing nicer than a lady riding side-saddle with a top hat and veil – very pleasing to the eye, especially for the male members of society looking on.

---

 top tip To protect your top hat on rainy days (they are made of cardboard and do not mix well with water), spray from a distance with a small amount of any silicone-based furniture polish. Then, using a silk scarf, gently rub around the hat in the direction of the silk itself. This will also help protect dressage hats.

top tip Always keep your top hat wrapped in a silk scarf and placed in a proper hatbox. Never ever put it in a plastic bag. Remember that silk is a natural material and needs to breathe. For this reason beware of using a new plastic or nylon hatbox. If this is the only choice available, leave the lid open when you have the hat stored at home.

top tip If you are unlucky enough to get your topper wet, stuff it with newspaper and dry well, away from direct heat.

Velvet safety hats

These are the posh hunt caps with all the safety features included. They are super useful for the child rider and the riding club adult. They double up for jumping but are not recommended for cross-country. Blue and black velvet are the most common. Browns and greens are available and may suit a particular colour combination;

we personally prefer the more traditional hues.

Tradition is so important if you really want to get it right. This type of hat also comes in a less shaped version, which sadly can make the wearer's head look rather big. This version is fine for hacking out but the overall appearance is somewhat clumsy and the dark straps hide the face.

 top tip Store your velvet safety hat the same way as any other velvet hat.

 top tip Always make sure that a trained person fits the hats to you. Never buy a hat from a friend. It may have been badly dropped or, worse still, the previous owner may have had a fall while wearing it. As with all safety hats, one bad fall and out they go. At the least get them checked by the manufacturers for cracks or weaknesses in the skull. These are not always easy to feel or see by the untrained eye.

 top tip Look out for flesh-coloured or light-coloured leather straps. These give a much better overall look to any rider and are so much more comfortable to wear.

● a smart hat with flesh-coloured three-point harness, so much more flattering than dark straps

● this is the same hat on two different shaped heads, showing just how important a mirror is!

Skull caps

Never the most flattering of items, but a must for the cross-country rider. They are generally quite comfortable and nowadays are made of lightweight materials. The choice of hat cover or silk is down to you, and black or navy velvet is an option. This is a good all-round hat and, because you can change the cover, it can be multi-purpose and safe. There are usually some great cover designs to be found during the Christmas period, and it is not unusual to see Rudolph trotting by on a pony in December. These hats are also good for everyday wear, when wet, only the cover will suffer. High visibility covers are also available. This type of hat is particularly favoured by event riders as they can wear the same hat in all three disciplines.

● skull cap with fitted velvet cover the correct size for the hat

top tip Always make sure you buy the correct-sized cover for your skullcap. Too big and you are in danger of losing it and looking like an egghead, or being blinded by it. Too small and you may look as though you are about to run in the 3.30 at Towcester racecourse.

top tip When going cross-country with fancy coloured silks on, avoid losing your hat cover by attaching strings through the harness to the silk. Not long ago hat silks were made with these. At least if it does come off the hat, it will stay attached, and you won't have to walk the course again to find it.

Air-vented hats

Known as the show-jumper's hat, this has become very popular with both aspiring young and not-so-young show jumpers, hoping to become a Whitaker. The designs have now been improved, and a lot of people find them comfortable and lightweight. Due to

advancements in the materials used, these hats have no sign of any velvet anywhere near them. This makes them great for everyday wear, especially in wet weather, as there is nothing to ruin. Sadly, because they are so untraditional, they are not a good choice for the show ring or dressage arena. They are sure to remain popular for riders less concerned with old-style etiquette.

● air-vented hat – another popular choice

top tip Wear these in the shop longer than you would do normally when trying on a hat. Some of them have a very square-shaped front that may result in a terrible headache and numbness of the forehead after a while.

grooms at shows

Oh dear, oh dear! Grooms' dress is the one area that is most complained about by show officials and competitors alike. The strange thing is, we really do not understand why people get it so wrong! At a school where a uniform is provided, do you see kids wearing something totally different? Is it acceptable that they do? The answer is an obvious 'no'. Is it possible that because there is not a set uniform, but a dress code, people decide just not to bother? Or is it because they do not understand the meaning of the term 'dress code'? There is no need to go anywhere with dirty clothes on, so why do people choose to put themselves on display in the ring looking so dishevelled?

In our opinion, this shows a total lack of respect – for the judge, the show officials, and the spectators.

A dress code allows you freedom to choose and work within it – but please do not ignore it completely. If you elect to do so, you may find that you will suffer the consequences. Such is the disregard for correct dress that some horse shows now 'police' the grooms coming into the ring. This is, of course, a total waste of time for the poor steward involved, and creates waves of tension when anyone is denied entry to the ring. We wonder whether it is just that everything is so much more casual these days that people actually do not know how to dress properly.

Not so long ago jeans were not something you would wear out

● left: would you accept a light, let alone a leg-up, from this man?

● nice colour co-ordination, but not quite smart enough!

to dinner but, when dressed up with a crisp white shirt and a smart jacket, the overall picture is good. Sadly this type of clothing has come in for so much abuse that denims are banned in many rings. Wearing a smart jacket with a T-shirt emblazoned with 'Sex Kitten' across the chest is not appropriate in the show ring either. Some shows are also insisting that people handling horses have to wear a safety hat at all times. Many grooms are to be seen wearing hunting caps but technically these are not safety hats – another occasion for checking the rules.

● easy wear, at home or away, for the showing mother

So, please, whenever you go into the ring with a horse, be aware, as always, of what you look like!

You can be smart, neat and tidy without incurring huge expense. A tweed jacket is a wonderful option – it's always smart and doesn't show the dirt easily. Add to this a blouse or shirt, cotton trousers and a hat – and away you go! Is it really so hard to keep up a standard? After all, when you are attending a well-turned-out horse, you should look good yourself.

The ring of a mobile phone is not a popular sound, especially in the ring. Either switch off or put it on 'vibrate' (much more fun!). If you do have to carry one, make sure it is not obvious, either ruining the line of your jacket or sticking out of your top pocket.

● very correct and very smart, but needs to carry his grooming kit at all times to avoid being mistaken for an official by the public and being asked the way to the loos!

● a smartly dressed groom ready for action, without bringing a suitcase into the ring!

top tip Keep life simple: one pair of blue, black or brown cotton trousers should go with most tweed jackets. A neat shirt or blouse, tucked in, will create a workman-like image. To finish it off, add an appropriate hat.

top tip All the above applies equally to men, but trilby hats, flat caps and bowlers are the more correct option. A tie should also be worn.

top tip This may not come as a surprise to some, but a baseball cap is not what the organisers think of as being a hat! Don't wear it or you may be refused entry into the ring.

top tip If the rules permit, and you would prefer to wear a fashionable hat rather than a safety hat, trot off to the charity shops again. They always seem to have hats and, of course, they will cost you a fraction of the normal price. Beware of the size of the brim, secure with a large hat pin, thus preventing the hat from leaving the ring before you do.

top tip Ladies, if you wish to wear a skirt, think again – they are not really practical. If you choose to do so, make sure that your footwear is suitable and that the length of skirt, coupled with choice of fabric, will survive an updraft or you bending over to oil the horse's hooves. You do not want to become the main attraction (if you do, please read the earlier chapter on choice of underwear).

top tip Gentlemen, if you choose to wear a skirt, please stay at home!

top tip When going to a show, do not forget the wet weather gear. You may find that a waxed long coat will suit you best at this time. If it is really wet underfoot, wellies or similar waterproof boots will be suitable. After all, you have to be dry to be comfortable.

nine | *on and off the horse*

Never before has there been such a wonderful array of fashions and colours, all designed to be worn on a horse, and which look equally good about town. Today's fast pace of living does not always give us the time to 'un-horse' ourselves after riding. Our children have always found it very embarrassing to be met at the school gate by a mother who looks as if she has left the horse in the car park or just fallen out of a bale of hay. Equally so, respect is not commanded when talking to the mother-in-law! Thankfully, this can be a thing of the past.

Modern clothing is user-friendly and easy to care for. There is little excuse for being seen anywhere in public in filthy clothes. Virtually all garments are now washing-machine friendly and will dry overnight with a little help from a radiator. The selection and drop in price of quality goods also means that owning just one decent coat is a thing of the past, enabling all of us to have one in the wash and one clean. For those instructing, three coats might be necessary so you can keep a clean one in the car. This will smarten up your appearance instantly, but remember that it must be a coat you can ride in. In all walks of life presentation makes a difference, and being dirty and smelling of horses will not impress your clients.

Not so long ago if you took a camera shot across a gathering at

● below: easy change for the busy mum, leaving her smart for shopping

● above: has anyone seen my horse? I must have left it in the car park

a British/European equestrian event such as Badminton Horse Trials, you would see green – not only a large portion of this green and pleasant land, but also a sea of green garments. The equestrian fraternity had a passion for the colours green or brown; maybe this was something to do with 'earth' colours? They wore these colours day in, day out, but never more so than when in the 'country'. These colours were very practical, as they did not show the dirt. The wearer blended into the countryside and could look very smart – but, my goodness, it all got so boring. And the more it was seen, the more it spread. It became infectious, multiplying with each event until it eventually broke the barriers and got out of control. Eventually it hit the cities, and nowhere was safe from the green welly, the green and brown moleskin or corduroy trousers, the cashmere jumper and the ultimate wax coat. These were shortly

● warming up at a show with a dual-purpose jacket – very smart when worn in the bar later!

joined by the nylon quilted, rather shapeless jacket available in moss green or navy, with knitted cuffs, itself then overtaken by the duck-down filled jacket in country tones. How unexciting, but very traditional and practical.

So what is new? And are we complaining? Not at all.

In recent years, manufacturers have introduced real colour into riding wear, and what a palette! In a slow move away from safe, dull colours we witnessed the introduction of navy, red and vibrant green. Checks became popular and could even be quite flattering. Then latterly manufacturers decided that pastels were the order of the day – very pretty and summery, but not very practical when holding a slobbery horse.

The choice is now vast and will continue to expand, using

colours that have never been seen around a horse before; fabric design has never been stronger . . . but such a huge choice can lead to more errors in what not to wear!

For your feet

Footwear for horse people has become so stylish and comfortable that it is not uncommon to see people wearing their short boots to go out in during the day and down to the pub in the evening. If you do choose to do this, please remember to clean them first! Days spent around horses tend to be long, so comfort is important.

When riding and working around horses it is recommended that you wear safe and correct boots to ensure that, when mounted, your feet do not slip through the stirrups and, when dismounted, your feet do not get squashed when being stepped on by a horse. (It's amazing how horses, being otherwise sensitive creatures, seem to go completely numb (and deaf) while standing on the human foot!) There are arguments for and against the use of steel toecaps. Some say that if the steel toecap got crushed onto your toes, you could lose them; others say they are a godsend. The decision is yours.

The boots on offer are amazing in their variety and appearance. Some give extra support around the ankle; some offer support to the foot arch. Whatever boots you choose, the fit is important, so walk around in them in the shop and at home. Remember also that new soles can behave like skis on certain horsebox ramps, so wear them in. Any boot with thick soles and deep treads will give you good grip on a stirrup, especially one with a rubber stirrup tread.

Paddock boots can have elastic sides, laces or zip-up fronts. They do fit differently and can be worn alone under trousers, or with half chaps or gaiters.

Some boots boast waterproof qualities – always handy on a wet day or when up early with morning dew. To prevent the 'cold trench' foot syndrome, rubber over-shoes or galoshes can be worn over boots, and indeed long boots when walking a course in wet going. We came across one lady rider judge who wore black knee-high socks over her boots when walking around the show ground prior to judging. While looking very strange, she did at least have clean boots to ride in. A novel way of protecting your boots.

If the flat boot is not your cup of tea, you could go up a step! One of us, being slightly shorter than the other, prefers to have a heel when on the ground. Enter, cowboy boots, which are now

girlie wellies, all spotty and pink

more popular than ever, having made a great come-back in the UK. We prefer the traditional leather colours – but, yes, you've got it, they are now available in blues and pinks and virtually any other colour you can imagine. These boots are very practical, tough and comfortable and will last forever. One important thing is to make sure of the leg fitting, so you not only look cool but can also ride comfortably. The fashion lookalikes available in the high street are rarely up to the rigours of everyday equestrian wear.

Other boots that have become popular are a combination

• colour coordination with toning hat for shows or smartening up at home; note zipped front boots

of leather and Gortex, a good practical mix and very stylish. An ad promoting these shows someone standing in a trough of water and drinking a glass of champagne. Understandably, the advertisers have found a captive market.

In this green and wet land, we cannot leave out wellies! We love them, and could not live without them. Originally black and then in oh-so-popular green, they really started a trend in rubber footwear. Navy blue wellies, red and then yellow followed – useful if you wanted to look like Paddington Bear or were lost in the mud. So what came next? Pink and sky blue with yellow spots, stars, stripes, flowers and other pastel colours. The rubber welly boot has never had it so good and has never been so fashionable. And, heaven forbid, is there more? Yes, we have zebra stripes, leopard prints, even silver and gold. From being necessary wet weather wear they are now the most sought-after, must-have, fashion accessory. But beware – as, glorious as they are, feet are still very, very vulnerable in them.

Trainers really are a no-no. Many people find them comfortable, and although available in leather, they still offer no protection and are hugely unsuitable to ride in.

Whatever your choice, you are now able to have smart, good-looking footwear that does a job, whether keeping you warm and dry, or protecting your feet from your horses' hooves. So let's move on to some of the not-so-clever objects that horse people choose for their feet! Clogs might be fantastic to wear, and are practical to a degree, but they are very easy to step out of. An embarrassing moment for one of us occurred when trotting a horse up for inspection. The horse ended up wearing the right clog. The mark is still on the wearer's heel and the horse has been sold to Holland!

Sights at shows are endless. A high heel or stiletto teetering in the mud has been seen all too often, and shown very little sympathy. What a surprise! And believe it or not, the Jesus sandal has been seen around lorry parks and collecting rings, sometimes with socks and sometimes without. They are definitely not recommended and highly un-chic.

● what we do not want to see near horses' hooves

top tip Keep an instant shoe-cleaning sponge in the car or some saddle-soap equivalent in a tub. A quick rub over will hide a multitude of sins whether you are going on to do the shopping or teaching after collecting a horse from a muddy field.

● aprés ride, keeping warm and dry and looking smart when away from the horse

Hats

Keeping your hair neat and tidy while mucking out a stable on a windy, rainy day has never been an easy task. Certainly any hair that falls over your face at this time will suffer from your dirty hands pushing it back into place. It is far better to tie it back or to wear a cap to hold it out of the way. Head scarves are no longer *de rigueur* for keeping hair under control; and there is only one lady in Britain who can get away with it while riding!

A cap is also a handy item to pop on after you have prepared your hair for the ring and do not wish to be seen wearing just your hairnet. This also means that you can work on your own turn-out

top tip

Always dry your leather hat away from direct heat.

> *top tip* Softer, waterproof hats can be washed on a 'delicates' cycle in the washing machine. To re-proof against the rain buy some spray-on rug re-proofer.

well ahead of time and then address the horses. The baseball cap is here to stay and is a handy addition to prevent sun-bleached hair and sun-stroke. Shading for the eyes is a welcome extra on long hot days.

For keeping your head dry, there is no longer a need to be cloned in the same in old wax hats. You can now buy a wonderful variety of colours, shapes and designs that all have the ability to keep your head dry and give you an individual look. This opportunity also provides you with the ability to colour co-ordinate your wet-weather hat with your other chosen clothing. If you are lucky enough to have a choice of coats, you may find that the leather bush hats will suit all of them, and look smart whatever you are going to do. These wonderful, long-lasting hats are also unisex so, as long as your heads are the same size, you can share them with your male friends.

Coats and waistcoats

Coats now come in all different shapes and colours. It is worth remembering your body shape before you buy a coat, whether it is to wear on or off a horse. The shorter blouson jackets look fantastic as long as there is no part of your body below the waist and above your knees that you wish to hide! For the slimmer person, whether male or female, these jackets look really great.

They are not the best in cold weather, though, particularly when riding – they tend to move up, leaving your bottom rather exposed to the elements. The same is true when wearing them in rain; and when off a horse they allow the water to run off onto the bottom of your waist and below – not very nice! On taller men they often appear too short; and it is worth remembering that one size up from your normal will allow more ease of movement in the elasticated waist area. As these jackets are quite fitted, pay attention to the

smart yet
practical

room you have across the
shoulders. Often this can be a
little tight and not allow the
freedom you need for a fast
muck-out and sweep-up.
Longer jackets cover up parts
you would rather others do not
see, plus giving you more
coverage against the weather.

**Many of the longer
jackets** have the facility to
be pulled in at the waist via
elastic inside the coat, and this
really does make a difference
and give you more shape. Do
be aware of the length: there is
nothing worse than sitting on
the back of the jacket all the
time when riding, and this will
also encourage the rain to go
under your seat and onto the

breathable
jacket with under-
layers for warmth

• waistcoats –
useful at any time

saddle. As said before, riding in wet undies is not to be recommended! Most of the longer jackets have insets in the sides at the bottom of the jacket. These jackets are worth spending the extra money on as they can be worn without the dangers mentioned above. Three-in-one jackets are available, but a good and sometimes cheaper alternative is to buy a separate waistcoat.

Waistcoats are one of the most useful items in our wardrobes. Made in different weights and fittings they need not make you resemble Michelin Man any more. They are handy for keeping you warm and can dramatically smarten up a plain outfit.

For warmer days out riding, the lightweight waistcoat is a must for keeping your mobile phone safe. The waistcoat is also a great friend to the larger individual and for those who feel self-conscious about their figure, the fitted waistcoat is an absolute must. They cover and hold together the wobbly bits, minimise bust bounce and neatly cover the bottom. Whatever coat or waistcoat you choose make sure, by looking in the mirror, that it is flattering.

When trying a coat or jacket, sit on a saddle horse. This will allow you to see where the jacket ends in relation to the back of the saddle. Equally so, with the help of a friend, you will get some

● not practical in colour or shape

● more flattering, and an easier garment for most to wear

indication of what the jacket does to you from the side view. If you plan to use the jacket while you are having lessons, you do not want the instructor to be unable to determine whether you are sitting up straight because your jacket is too bulky. Lighter colours are fun, but they will show the dirt and in some cases accentuate your size.

Keeping warm is essential and it is worth remembering to leave room for extra layers under a winter jacket. Riding, or for that matter doing anything in a jacket which is too tight, is not going to help your performance or comfort factor. The use of breathable materials is a huge plus. All too often we have gone out on a cold day on the horses and after the first trot have realised we are over-dressed. The breathable garments are great when unzipped at this point and prevent less sweating for the male rider and less glowing from the female!

top tip If you want to wear duck down and cannot cope with the washing problems, choose a waistcoat. These generally require fewer visits to the washing machine and do make a huge difference in keeping you warm.

top tip To fluff up your duck down, place two tennis balls (not the ones your dog plays with) into the tumble drier. This tried-and-tested method is now included in some of the washing instructions for these clothes.

top tip Choose a colour that goes with all your other riding clothes. Some jackets come in lovely colours but are hard to match with other riding clothes.

top tip Remember, your coat is a working garment, so make sure it can cope with the punishment you are going to give it and the dirt you are going to get on it.

top tip Lighter weight materials can blow around more in the breeze. Beware of the fabric used: anything that rustles or crackles may well leave you grounded!

top tip Be seen, be safe! You no longer have to look like a road maintenance worker while riding on the roads. There are now jackets that are much easier to wear in both colour and material that will make you visible to traffic. Retro-reflective strips or circles are brilliant – they appear as grey metallic in daylight, but after dark, when caught in lights, they give out a bright reflection.

top tip Gloves are just as important off the horse as on. They protect your nail varnish and save injury to the hands and nails!

● be seen, be safe
– jacket with
reflective circles on
the cuffs

The jackets that keep you really warm are filled with duck
down. We both feel that these are fantastic for teaching and wearing
at shows, on cold but fair days, but not so user-friendly to work in.
Due to the bulk of the duck down they do not suit all shapes and
sometimes make people look like body builders – great for the men
but not so good for the ladies. They require more care and looking
after when placed near a washing machine and do not take kindly
to getting overly rained on. The wrong washing and drying
techniques can ruin one of these jackets – an expensive mistake
many of us have made. There is an art to their care and it is worth
following the manufacturer's washing instructions to the letter. If not
dried correctly they can omit a rather nasty whiff that any wet dog,
or duck, would be proud of! Having said all of that, they do their
job well and not only keep you warm but also can double up as a

● fun, funky clothes
for the smaller
people in your life

ski jacket on that winter trip to Klosters.

Wet weather days are a pain for the horse rider and
owner. Cold, wet days are even less popular. The good old waxed
coat or long mac certainly has done its job over time but there are
easier garments to work in now. The most common complaint
regarding the wax jacket is how hot it is to work and ride in, so
again we look to our breathable materials. There is also the amount
of time that the wax takes to dry out (and the smell, both before and
after) making it a less popular garment than it used to be. Oddly
enough with all these factors we still think that on the very worst
wet weather day they keep you drier than anything else, and if the
long version is worn with wellies, legs stay dry too.

> ***top tip*** Check out local retailers rather than a saddlery shop to buy fleeces. With a bit of thought you may be able to colour co-ordinate them with your breeches and coat and not spend as much money.

> ***top tip*** Never clip a horse in a fleece. Once done never forgotten, as the short hairs are stuck in forever. Certain fleeces attract shavings and hay, even without you having had a roll in them!

> ***top tip*** Fleeces with collars that zip right up to the neck are a wonderful warmer in the worst days of winter. There is nothing better than a warm neck to make you feel toasty all over. This advice applies to children as well.

> ***top tip*** Hoodies are not a good option. They are not practical and have a life of their own at faster paces, when they act as an unwelcome windsock.

> ***top tip*** Jackets and waistcoats should be fastened at all times to avoid spooking the horse. When blowing in the wind they may appear like a ship in full sail.

Layers

One thing is for sure, the sweater is out and the fleece is in! Fleeces can be found at all different prices, in every colour of the rainbow and are easy to wash and look after. Saddlery shops will provide you with so many different types that a short shopping trip may develop into a long one. Once again, the fit is all-important, especially as you are now able to buy shaped fleeces and these certainly get rid of the baggy look. Whereas many people think that baggy is good to hide what lies beneath, it can actually add to the problem. Resembling a colourful sack is unnecessary and can make you look unkempt. Another frequent problem with the long and baggy is the possibility of being hooked onto the back of the saddle. Believe us, it does happen! The prices vary dramatically and this is one area where the designer label commands a higher price. There is no doubt that in this range quality can last longer and wash better, but generally these garments are hassle free to wash and dry. For those of us less good at following washing instructions they are also, thank goodness, really hard to shrink. It is now possible to colour coordinate your jacket to your fleece or to your waistcoat, and this also provides an outfit nice enough to be seen at any chilly summer barbecue. Never before has any garment been quite so useable and wearable on and off the horse. Most clothing companies have added to the range with the provision of matching polo and rugby shirts

● coats of many colours – practical use of layers, fantastic for warmth

and, worn with the corresponding breeches or jodhpurs, an amazing outfit can be seen.

T-shirts are not always the best option for riding, especially for ladies over a UK size 12. We both feel that the polo shirt, with a collar, is a much more flattering choice. These are easy to find and do not have to be purchased from saddlery shops. In fact they are now so common that you can even pick them up at your local supermarket. For the fuller figure these shirts are easily worn without being tucked in, always a bonus. With a waistcoat over the top for the cooler days, the rider can look smart at all times. Riding and getting a full tan on the arms and not the brown glove look, as seen on a lot of riders, is also an option, as these shirts come with no sleeves. Do, however, watch out for low branches as they can give you nasty scratches. It is also worth remembering that you may not have your sun cream handy and burnt shoulders are painful. As for strappy tops and boob tubes – darlings, we would rather not go there!

Trousers and leg wear

As we have said in another chapter, breeches and jods can be worn well with boots, half or full chaps. If you do not want to wear riding breeches, there are other options, which can be practical, comfortable and smart. Riding trousers used to be rather butch and did little to flatter the figure or excite the imagination. Moleskin, needlecord or twill were the only choices.

Equestrian manufacturers now produce a good range of trousers, using cotton, Lycra and elastane. Most of these have a jean-type design and straight leg. The most important point to bear in mind with trousers is the cut. As with breeches, high-waisted can be uncomfortable on certain shapes and low-waisted can be just too revealing. The seat area needs to be comfortable for riding, so take note of where the seams are! If in the wrong place you could get rather uncomfortable. Again, look at the inner leg seams. Originally the best jeans came from America, and some would say they still do. A certain brand had only single seams on the inside leg for non-chafing, and double seams on the outer. In Britain a new breed of

● same trousers, same legs, different uses

riding jean appeared on the market some time ago. These were with a full leg and seat inset made of a form of vinyl, designed to look like leather, but certainly not having the same feel. Their best attribute was to stick you onto the trickiest of horses but not recommended to be worn on a hot day or on heated seats in the car!

Boot-cut trousers may look good with cowboy boots off a horse, but be sensible either on or around a horse – you do not need to be seen in full flight with a gale blowing up your leg because your flares are too wide. It is possible to buy riding trousers with a small flare and zip up the side of the leg. Un-zipped these give a boot-cut appearance, and while zipped up they fit under a boot. (Under your boot or half chap the zip may be a problem, but they make a stylish change for the younger rider.)

 top tip Body shape is all-important. Remember this when buying trousers.

 top tip Make sure you have enough knee room to ride in if you want dual-purpose leg wear.

 top tip Stretch trousers are easier to ride and work in as they provide you with that extra bit of 'give'.

Neat, straight-cut trousers are what we recommend, but, most importantly, they must be worn at the correct length.

If worn too short, your trousers look as if they have had an argument with your boots, and when astride, they will allow either a glimpse of sexy ankle or not-so-sexy sock. If the trouser is worn too long, you end up wearing half the showground on your hem, and the popular sloppy, street-look simply does not work with horses.

Too tight a trouser looks hideous on a larger person, so do look at your rear view in the mirror – and, yes, you do need to be able to bend down and pick things up from ground level. The placing of pockets and zips can improve the fit of trousers, and while some pockets are useful, side pockets do not help anyone.

Waists with an elastic insert we like, and can be a complete godsend. You can still wear a size 12 even if you're a size 14! Simply hide the waistband with a belt and you look good and feel comfortable.

Colours are your choice, but what you are wearing on your top half, what you are doing, and the weather, all play a part. Pale cream trousers on a muddy wet day do not look good when splattered with mud or covered in paw marks where the dog has jumped up.

Moleskin trousers and cords are still great, being very practical and easy to wear. (No, we do not mean real moleskins!) Men and ladies can wear these and look very country and correct. And, men, let's not forget you. The choice of colours in cotton and cord trousers is truly amazing, ranging from earth colours to navy and red. And now, can you believe, lemon, pink and purple? Patterned handkerchiefs and striped socks are then the order of the day to complete the ensemble. Pleats can be a good friend or a bad enemy. To know which one it is, go back to the mirror and be honest. The slimmer and taller the man, the easier it is to wear front pleats and look good. Larger and rounder gentlemen look neater in flat-fronted trousers; this second rule applies also to the ladies. Going back to the men, we still linger over the back view, so use mirrors please and, yes, there is nothing better than the tightest pale moleskins on a neat bum, à la Crocodile Dundee!

colour coordinating with your horse

Whatever discipline you choose, nothing can beat a tidy, correct and workmanlike turn-out. A well-fitted hacking jacket accompanied by a good shirt and tie will never let you down. Presenting yourself correctly will give you the confidence to do the job well.

In the hat department we have always preferred navy blue as it goes with every colour, other than black, and is less severe.

As ever, check the rules of each competition – canary and yellow breeches are not usually seen in the dressage/show-jumping ring.

horse	jacket	shirt	tie	breeches	boots
CHESTNUT	Brown tweed (light or dark), can include orange/greens in the weave pattern, or a green tweed (dark or light) with either darker green or brown in the weave pattern.	Pale lemon, green or cream; can include small stripe to compliment the weave of the jacket. Pinks are not a good option.	With a brown tweed select a brighter red base with a darker spot stripe, or, for the less bold, a darker base colour with a red spot/stripe. With green tweed select a pale base colour, e.g. lemon, with a darker green spot/stripe or the reverse.	All colours suit, but canary is good, especially on liver chestnuts.	Black or brown – brown can make a stylish difference. Kids: brown jod boots.
BAY	Brown tweed (light or dark) with red or green weave pattern, or green tweed with brown or grey weave pattern. Dark bays look better with lighter-coloured browns and greens.	Pastel colours, including a small cream stripe if desired. Pinks can be worn with the darker brown, as long as there is not too much red in the weave.	Decide on the shirt colour first and match the base colour of the tie, then look for a spot or stripe to pick up the colours in the weave pattern of jacket. If wearing a pastel pink shirt, choose a darker base-coloured tie with a hint of pink/green in the pattern.	All will look good but bright canary is too much.	Black or brown. Kids: brown jod boots.

horse	jacket	shirt	tie	breeches	boots
GREY	Grey tweed with a blue weave pattern/blue velvet collar; green tweed (darker) with a blue/grey weave pattern; or if a rose/roan grey mid-brown tweed with a grey weave pattern. Blue tweed can look OK but check the quality of the cloth.	Pastel blues and pinks, with or without stripe, or beige with cream or grey stripe to match the brown tweed. A white coloured shirt on a white-grey tones in well.	Pastel blue and pink shirts require a more dominant base colour – choose a darker blue or dark pink with a spot or stripe of the same colour in a lighter tone.	Steer clear of bright canary at all times, and pale lemon if wearing grey tweed, but all other colours suit.	Black, or brown if worn with brown tweed. Kids: brown jod boots darkened with polish.
SKEWBALD	Brown or green tweeds with a grey/red/orange pattern weave. If grey and white refer to greys. Beware of loud check patterns when riding colourful horses.	Pastel lemons and greens, with a cream/white stripe and white collar (optional).	Keep it plain – you have enough colour already! With the lemon shirt wear a green tie, and with the green wear a lemon tie. Spots and stripes are OK but in suitable similar colours.	Most suit, but bright canary is not good against a predominantly white horse.	Black or brown; brown is good on a brown and white horse. Kids: brown jod boots.
PIEBALD	Green tweed with darker green weave pattern, or darker grey tweed with a darker weave pattern, or a lighter blue/grey weave pattern. Brown can also be worn but is better with a blue/grey weave pattern or a red weave pattern.	Soft lemon with the green tweed, and pastel or light blue with the brown tweed, with or without cream/white stripe and white collar.	Keep it plain! Take the colour of the weave pattern in your coat and match to it. A subtle spot or stripe may be OK, but do not go mad.	Canary breeches are a bad idea; pale lemon if subtle is ok, but a softer, neutral colour is best.	Black. Kids: brown jod boots, polished with darker polish to tone down.
STRAWBERRY ROAN	This colour carries a lot of brown in it, so check out bays (opposite); but as they also have grey in the coat, you can add grey/blue to the weave pattern.	Match the shirt to the weave pattern colour and think of the pastels, especially a pink with grey/blue weave pattern.	Darker, plainer ties look best, even a brown with cream spot.	Canary is good with the browner tweeds but not so attractive with the grey/blue weave pattern. Lemon is always a good option.	Black, or brown (very classy on this colour). Kids: brown jod boots.
PALOMINO	Brown tweed with reds/oranges or a hint of gold/yellow in the pattern; greens with a brown or burgundy/brown pattern weave.	Lemons and creams with red/brown stripe or plain. No pinks.	Reds with yellow/gold small spots.	Canary through to neutral.	Black or brown. Kids: brown jod boots.

horse	jacket	shirt	tie	breeches	boots
BLACK	Beware: darker colours will disappear into the horse of this colour. Lighter browns with a darker blue/grey weave, greens with the same weave pattern or a hint of red can lift the picture.	Go for bright and bold. Strong yellow, cornflower blue, or cream with a stronger stripe to pick up the colour of the weave pattern.	Match the tie to your shirt colour, but take the shade down or up to really contrast. Stripe or spot is fine, but stick to neutral colours.	Pale lemon or cream; canary is just a little too much.	Black. Kids: brown jod boots polished with darker boot polish to tone down.
BROWN/DUN	Dark browns should refer to the bay section. Lighter browns and duns should look to brown with red/orange weave pattern, or green with brown weave pattern.	Lemon comes top with these colours, but brown can carry a soft red/pink when worn with brown tweed with red weave pattern.	Any red with a small check or stripe in cream with the brown tweed, and lemon with the green tweed.	Canary or pale lemon is a must; beige tends to pale away.	Black or brown. Kids: brown jod boots.
APPALOOSAS AND SPOTS	Check out your spot colours and then decide which colour dominates. Generally there is a lot of brown in the coat, so look at the bay section. If you have a black leopard spot stick to darker green tweed with a hint of blue in the pattern weave.	Plain pastels, lemons, pinks, blues or cream with a fine darker beige or brown stripe.	Strong, plain colours to match the chosen shirt. Keep patterns to a minimum.	The more coloured horse can carry a paler canary, but otherwise stick to very pale lemon or beige.	Black or brown (if not a black leopard spot). Kids: brown or darkened brown jod boots.